FORTUNE-TELLING

with

PLAYING CARDS
TAROT CARDS
DICE

DIAMOND
BOOKS

Diamond Books
An Imprint of HarperCollins*Publishers*
77-85 Fulham Palace Road,
Hammersmith, London W6 8JB

The material in this book is taken from
The Aquarian Book of Fortune-Telling, © The Aquarian Press, 1987;
Tarot in Action!, © Sasha Fenton, published by The Aquarian Press 1987;
and *Fortune-Telling by Dice*, © David and Julia Line,
published by The Aquarian Press 1984.

1 3 5 7 9 10 8 6 4 2

A catalogue record for this book is available from the British Library

ISBN 0 261 66774 2

Printed in Great Britain

All rights reserved. No part of this publication may be
reproduced, stored in a retrieval system, or transmitted,
in any form or by any means, electronic, mechanical,
photocopying, recording or otherwise, without the prior
permission of the publishers.

CONTENTS

PART ONE

FORTUNE-
TELLING

with

PLAYING CARDS

1
HOW TO CONSULT THE CARDS

A successful reading depends on a truly representative selection of cards chosen by the questioner and the ability of the interpreter to understand them. The questioner and the interpreter may be one and the same person because we most certainly can read our own cards, but an assistant will always give a much more objective assessment of the situation.

The first qualification necessary to become a good cartomancer is a genuine desire to do so! This, backed up with plenty of enthusiasm and lots of practice is all that is needed to succeed. If there is a 'feeling' for the cards then so much the better. Although meanings of individual cards are readily available, it is the intuitive association and linking together of these that gives depth to the over-all message. A psychic and sensitive nature is an advantage, but this is something that actually develops through working with the cards in their oracular capacity.

When first learning to read the cards use nothing more than their basic meanings. This will give an over-all message and assessment of a situation although it may appear somewhat stilted. Remembering that 'practice makes perfect', confidence is soon gained and the intuitive links between one card and another quickly develop.

The most difficult part of an interpretation is telling the questioner that obstacles are ahead, especially when that person is already in trouble. It helps to know that by doing this you are helping them to avoid a problem or, at the very least, saving them from being taken by complete surprise. It is essential that you offer hope where there is despair and give comfort in place of sorrow. Look for a solution, which can always be seen in the cards alongside the problem, rather like the healing dock being found next to the spiteful nettle. Again, practice is necessary to recognize these symbolic antidotes among the hurdles.

Traditional Rituals

There are traditional rituals involved in selecting and reading the cards which should be observed wherever possible. This helps to bring into play those synchronistic moments which allow the questioner, unconsciously, to select the right cards. It also increases the awareness of the interpreter and generally produces harmony between them and the cards.

Ideally, a new pack of cards should be purchased and kept solely for the purpose of divination. These should be handled only by yourself and questioners who select spreads from them for you to interpret. No games of any nature should ever be played with them.

Cards for divination should really be kept in a set place, preferably higher than table-top level. It is said this keeps them above mundane matters and the best place is the top shelf of a dark cupboard. True initiates of the cards advocate that a hand-sewn silk bag is made for them to which they are returned immediately after a reading. This is done to preserve their oracular power which increases with proper use. Mis-handling and using them for card games releases this energy with a result that their harmonies are disturbed, affecting both questioner and interpreter.

The Questioner and Interpreter

Before a spread can be chosen, questioners must decide whether they want a general reading or one that highlights a particular aspect of their life. If, for example, their concern is their love life then a spread suitable for this would be very different from one designed to give an over-all picture of their situation. Again, if a character analysis is required yet another spread would be preferred. The number of questions asked from a spread does not matter, although three is usual, so long as they relate to the subject in question.

It will also be necessary to choose a representative court card for some of the spreads. The secret of discovering the most appropriate one lies in assessing a personal standpoint in relation to a problem or situation, as described later in 'How to Choose a Court Card'.

Preparation for a Reading

Handling the cards is most important for it imprints them with personal vibrations. Before using new cards for a reading, shuffle and cut them as many times as possible and, whilst doing so, look closely at their intricate designs and numbers. The more you familiarize yourself with these the better they respond to your questions.

A relaxed atmosphere is essential when reading the cards. The burning of a joss-stick helps achieve this and so does a warm room rather than a cold one. From a purely practical point of view make sure that the table is large enough to accommodate the spread because if it is bunched up, continuity and expansion of thought are correspondingly hampered. If possible use a round table and then sit with your back to the North and have the questioner facing you with their back to the South.

Procedure

Before placing the pack of cards on the table the interpreter must shuffle them to rid them of any previous influence. If a court card is necessary to represent the questioner it is chosen at this stage, after the initial shuffling by the interpreter. Having decided on this it is then carefully placed to one side, ready to be included in the final selection.

The remaining 51 cards, or 52 cards if a court card is not necessary, are now handed to the questioner who, with the nature of their problem or situation clearly and uppermost in their mind, proceeds to shuffle them thoroughly. The cards are then ceremoniously placed in the centre of the table and are cut by the questioner three times with the left hand. (This hand is nearer the heart, both anatomically and emotionally).

Next, the interpreter picks them up and spreads them face downwards across the table, in a slightly overlapping line. They are now ready for the questioner to make a selection, the number of which will depend on the spread chosen for the reading. This selection is done completely spontaneously when it will be found that the eye leads the hand, the left hand, automatically to certain cards. As they are chosen they are removed and placed face downwards in a small pack, strictly in order of choice. When the required number has been extracted the remaining cards should be removed from the table.

Placing the Court Card

If the spread required a personal court card it is added by the questioner now. Keeping the selected cards face downwards so that their values are not revealed, the personal card is placed among them. This may be a random placing or a calculated, conscious decision as to where it is inserted; it may be exactly in the middle, the third, the ninth, the fifth position etc. This choice is entirely up to the questioner.

The interpreter now takes the selected cards, with or without the personal court card, in readiness to arrange them into a particular spread. At this point it may be necessary to turn the cards over so that the bottom card, the first one chosen, is at the top. This is most important if the cards are to be placed in order of selection.

When a satisfactory reading has been completed the cards are reunited into a full pack and thoroughly shuffled by the interpreter in order to disconnect them from present association. They are then returned to their secluded place of safety in readiness for the next reading.

2
THE MYSTICAL CROSS

This is a British spread originating from the Knights Templars. It gives us an excellent over-all assessment of a personal situation on all levels, indicating relationships between lovers, family, friends and acquaintances, career and business prospects, ambitions, money matters and the inevitable obstacles and hurdles in life too. It also shows individual characteristics and psychic potential so may also be used for a character study or psychic reading.

Method
A personal court card is necessary to represent the questioner, plus twelve more, making thirteen cards in all. Having carried out the ritualistic preparation and chosen the most appropriate court card, remove this from the pack. The remaining 51 cards are then spread face downwards across the table in a slightly overlapping line, by the interpreter. Twelve cards are selected from these by the questioner, who keeps them strictly in the order of selection. The court card is then placed significantly among them in the way previously described.

The interpreter now takes the thirteen cards and turns them face upwards, thus revealing the first card selected, and arranges them to form the equilateral cross as shown in Diagram 1 (on page 246).

The line down represents the present situation and the line across reflects influences which will affect this situation. The position of the court card is noted first. If this is in the line down, it shows the questioner's circumstances are likely to control them more than they are able to control their circumstances. If it is in the line across, then it means it is well within their power to control and influence matters. Should this court card be in the middle of the cross then the questioner is assured that the situation will shortly be resolved in a most satisfactory way.

The card in the centre of the cross is interpreted next. This indicates the major aspect around which everything revolves at present. It is both a cause and an effect, with its significance

11

depending on the suit and individual meaning of the card.

Cards in the line down are interpreted individually and linked together to symbolize aspects of the present situation. Finally, the cards in the line across are interpreted individually as influences which will alter the present situation in the future.

THE MYSTICAL CROSS

7 of spades
Queen of hearts
4 of clubs
2 of diamonds/7 of diamonds/9 of spades/4 of diamonds/3 of diamonds/5 of hearts/King of hearts
2 of spades
6 of hearts
8 of spades

Question: What does the future hold for me?

Court Card: Queen of hearts

Combinations and Relationships of the Cards:

Two Twos: Separate ways

Two Fours: Uncertainty at present

Two Sevens: Mutual Love

Position of the Court Card: This is in the line down showing that circumstances control the questioner more than she is able to control them.

The line down represents the present situation.

7 of Spades: The fact that this card heads this line indicates that personal fears and worries dominate the situation. Most of these will come to nothing but, even so, a shadow is cast over everything, producing apprehension and negativity.

Queen of Hearts: This court card represents the questioner. Her family, home and emotional happiness are her life. There seem to be worries on the one hand, 7 of spades, and money troubles on the other, 4 of clubs. 'Thinking' mainly with her heart, not her head, neither of these problems will be easily resolved.

4 of Clubs: This card warns of the loss of an asset. It might be a purse, key or other valuable personal possession but, at the same time, it also indicates difficulties to make ends meet financially.

4 of Diamonds: Much revolves around this card because it is in the centre of the cross. Practical problems are difficult to solve and communications with others seem to break down. Decision making is virtually impossible so this prolongs the issue.

2 of Spades: Two sides of the question are seen but both look equally

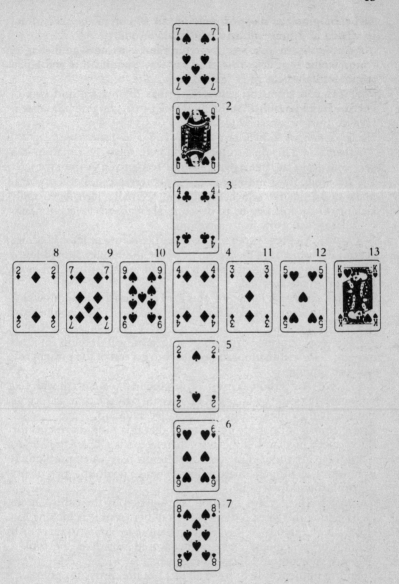

The Mystical Cross

bad. The practical decision reflected in the previous card comes to a head and steps will have to be taken soon.

6 of Hearts: Again, two sets of circumstances are at loggerheads. A compromise is going to be the only way out and this will entail considerable self-sacrifice, emotionally.

8 of Spades: A drain on resources brings depression and lack of energy. It is advisable that the questioner trusts no one but herself. Health must be watched carefully.

The line across reflects influences which will affect the present situation.

2 of Diamonds: This dual influence will help solve the situation in a very practical way, but its value is not recognized at the time.

7 of Diamonds: This influence represents the questioner's practical plans and initiative which, until now, seems to have been sadly lacking. Once this begins to develop, she can expect action. Self-confidence will grow from this point.

9 of Spades: Depressing though this influence is, at least it brings action. By seeing it as a necessary evil the questioner should know that the present is a stage which must be passed through before better times are reached.

4 of Diamonds: As an influence, this card emphasizes loyalties which conflict with what should be done. The head must rule over the heart in this instance.

3 of Diamonds: Practical drive and enthusiasm will develop with this influence. Determination, so necessary to get out of the present rut, will also emerge.

5 of Hearts: A decision to escape from the real issue is felt with this influence. Personal feelings will be overruled by the practical scene, but this is the only way out of a negative situation.

King of Hearts: It can only be assumed that this King represents the questioner's husband. If this is so, then he too is a 'heart-thinker' so is little help in producing a practical solution to his wife's problem. It is, however, a compassionate influence which no doubt gives plenty of comfort and love to her.

Conclusions: The present situation, symbolized by the cards, shows life is getting this person down. Much of her trouble is looking too closely and intently at herself in relation to circumstances. An unknowing selfishness exists which would vanish if she took a different view point of the whole scene.

Future influences help solve all this but the cards also point out that she needs to adopt a more practical approach to life in order to balance the emotional outlook she has at present.

3
THE PACK OF CARDS

Each card represents a different aspect, on different levels, of the over-all meaning of the suit to which it belongs. These are its numerical, practical, psychological, psychic, influential and reversed significances which depend on the spread and standpoint from which the cards were selected.

The twelve court cards represent people, as well as certain qualities, whereas the forty numbered cards symbolize situations and circumstances.

The Joker
This card finds its way into a spread in most surprising ways even though it is thought to have been previously removed. The fact that there is a Joker in the pack at all is significant in itself, so he cannot possibly be ignored. So if he does turn up unexpectedly, do not replace him with another card because his presence and message was intended.

Combinations and Relationships
Significant combinations and relationships of certain cards in a spread have collective meanings which give added insight into problems and situations. These are given in the following lists:

Quartets, Triplicities and Pairs
Four Aces   – Triumph
Three Aces   – Harmony
Two Aces   – Reunion
Four Kings   – Honour and success
Three Kings   – Good support
Two Kings   – Good advisers
Four Queens   – Scandal
Three Queens   – Gossip
Two Queens   – Curiosity

Four Jacks	– Battles
Three Jacks	– Quarrels
Two Jacks	– Discussions
Four Tens	– Change for the better
Three Tens	– Repayments
Two Tens	– Change of fortune
Four Nines	– Unexpected good fortune
Three Nines	– Successful enterprise
Two Nines	– Eventual contentment
Four Eights	– Worries
Three Eights	– Burdens lessen
Two Eights	– Inconstancy
Four Sevens	– Equality
Three Sevens	– Fulfilment
Two Sevens	– Mutual love
Four Sixes	– Unexpected obstacles
Three Sixes	– Hard work
Two Sixes	– Contradictions
Four Fives	– Personal happiness
Three Fives	– Personal satisfaction
Two Fives	– Personal uncertainty
Four Fours	– Equal chance
Three Fours	– A fair chance
Two Fours	– Little chance
Four Threes	– Hope
Three Threes	– Stability
Two Threes	– Choice
Four Twos	– Cross-roads
Three Twos	– Change in direction
Two Twos	– Separate ways
The Joker	– Be not deceived, this is an unknown quantity.

Significant Relationships

The ace of diamonds among several hearts	– Business and pleasure do not mix
The ace of diamonds among several clubs	– Matters of business depending on money will come to a head
The ace of spades among several hearts	– Emotional problems
The ace of spades among several diamonds	– Obstacles at work or with a career and ambition

The ace of hearts among several clubs	–	Generosity
The ace of hearts among several diamonds	–	Love and romance connected with a journey or work
The ace of clubs among several diamonds	–	Wealth and an increase of social status
The ace of clubs among several spades	–	Financial problems
A number of mixed court cards	–	Festivity, hospitality and social gatherings
A court card between two cards of the same number or value	–	Soemone is supported or hemmed in by their circumstances
A Jack next to a King or Queen	–	Protection
The Queen of spades between a King and another Queen	–	A break-up of a relationship
The eight and nine of spades together	–	A health problem
A Jack among several diamonds	–	A messenger will bring important information or news
The nine and ten of diamonds together	–	A journey on or over the sea
The nine of hearts and the three of diamonds together	–	A stable love-affair

DIAMONDS

ACE OF DIAMONDS

Numerical Significance

This is the first and last card in this suit and represents both numbers one and thirteen – unity and rebirth. It signifies a beginning and an end in itself, thus representing a complete project. In this lies an individual's potential and creativity, as expressed through the intellect. Intellectual striving, which should be directed towards one goal at a time, is necessary, even though the seed of success has been sown. This card also contains the power to transform one situation into another.

Practical Significance

In its purest sense this card symbolizes a clear-cut aim for the future. It is a veritable storehouse of energy, sufficient for putting into action all plans relating to practical and material goals. Like the diamond itself, ambitions should be crystallized, then a single-minded approach utilized to achieve these aims as soon as possible.

This card also signifies new business, a new house or new possession, such as a car, furniture or jewellery. An important document or letter which has the power to alter the future is also represented by this card. Such a communication may be sent or received; and those who have taken exams can expect favourable results. It also symbolizes the renewal of hope through intellectual concentration and a more positive attitude, thus encouraging those who have failed in the past to try again. Originality plus drive will bring practical success and material gain.

Psychological Significance

Tremendous drive and positivity produce a forceful character who means to reach his or her goal by hook or by crook. Crystal-clear thinking allows the individual to cut corners and take risks with safety. Unflagging energy and good health aid the attainment of the highest ambitions which others would see as remote castles in the air. A lack of feeling for others may be displayed as this would contribute little to furthering personal ambitions.

Psychic Significance

An occult achievement of some importance is on the cards. This is an initiation which marks a stage of positive psychic development. Inspirational qualities and telepathic gifts crystallize into rewarding experiences which, in turn, produce the confidence necessary for going on to the next phase. One cycle has been successfully completed and the scene is now set for the future.

Influential Significance

This card has a strong, positive influence enabling the individual to direct his or her forces towards the fulfilment of an aim. Businesses, careers and ambitions receive a boost of energy which revives enthusiasm and helps to bring things to a successful conclusion. This influence will override opposition, especially when the aim is for the good of others.

Reversed Signifcance

Generally this card indicates muddled plans for the future. Good intent remains, but does not receive the stimulation necessary to spark it off. Everything becomes a stumbling-block which over-shadows personal potential. A set-back is to be expected.

KING OF DIAMONDS

The King's Significance

This King represents the mature, masculine aspect of this suit. A

combination of experience and action will produce a break-through into new interests. Coming to terms with life has paid off, so the future holds out great promise. On the practical level, stability gives the questions the confidence to help others as well as to further personal aims. Crowned with success materially, a good basis exists on which to develop other characteristics symbolized by the other three suits.

Practical Significance

Traditionally, this King is the fair-haired, blue-eyed man, muscularly strong and essentially practical. He is a clear thinker who uses his head and prides himself on his successes in business and with women. It may signify lack of heart and little consideration for others. He is ambitious, reliable, generally honest and his life appears to be an open book. Really, there is more to him than this although it usually goes unnoticed.

This outward-going personality is naturally disciplined, so a military career would be most fulfilling. As a protector he can be authoritarian yet respected nevertheless. As a business partner he will prove loyal and hard-working, but as a marriage partner he needs to be top dog. Romance usually lasts just long enough to convince a woman that he has a heart – then his work takes first place in his life. Whatever else this King may be, he is an excellent business man.

Psychological Significance

Here is an extrovert who thinks almost exclusively with his head. Strength of character gives him figure-head qualities although this does not necessarily mean that his nature is entirely balanced. As his emotions tend to be inhibited he runs the risk of developing into a dogmatic leader. This characteristic becomes morre pronounced as the years go by.

Psychic Significance

As a potential magician this King could command and direct the positive forces of Nature for the good of others. Both as a healer and an occultist, his powers will depend on his personal level of understanding and, as he progresses in life and evolves, so will he increase his links with the universe.

Influential Significance

The personal influence from this card is strong and positive. It will persuade others to fall in with your ideas and help things to go to plan although over-enthusiasm and drive may be mistaken for ruthlessness. This influence will help all who are willing to accept hard, unsentimental advice.

Reversed Significance

Strong ambitions develop into devious schemes which eventually undermine stability and confidence. Others lose faith in this King and his plans, which the result that aggression creeps in. Disputes create further problems until the only solution lies in travel or moving to a new home.

QUEEN OF DIAMONDS

The Queen's Significance

This card represents the feminine aspect of the suit. She has a practical and fertile imagination which enables her to compete successfully in a man's world. Independence has been won and she is capable of making important decisions speedily and accurately, often to the annoyance of her contemporaries. A loyal supporter of authority, she is seen as a protective female rather than as a motherly soul. Her ambition is to maintain her well-earned position in life rather than to extend her horizons into unknown territory.

Practical Significance

Traditionally, this Queen has fair hair, blue eyes and a generally pale look. Be not deceived, however, because she is strong, both physically and mentally and knows her own mind. She often thinks she knows other people's too, and this gives her a reputation for being over-authoritative and bossy.

Thinking with her head more than her heart has won her a place in society and brought rewards. As a business woman she succeeds with ease. A career will tend to take precedence over her home and family in the end, although this Queen usually has both these aspects well under control. She is an efficient mother, firm but well-loved. Energy abounds and life always holds out the promise of adventure and change. Organization is second nature to her and demand for her services is therefore great. She is an efficient, positive woman.

Psychological Significance

An unusually positive streak gives this woman an extrovert personality similar to that of a man. Seeing the world as a practical playground, she uses her intelligence to work and play in the best places. Others are jealous of her, but she secretly envies them for their domesticity. As she is so business-like, she is often misjudged as a hard-hearted person.

Psychic Significance

Occult and healing abilities soon develop once this Queen has stepped onto the positive psychic path. Working slowly but surely, she learns to command the positive forces of nature and uses them to help mankind and all other forms of life on this planet.

Influential Significance

Personal influence amounts to self-confidence and self-reliance which, in turn, attracts both friends and hangers-on. These qualities have brought success in the past and will do so again in the future. Others may benefit from this Queen's experience if they take her advice, which is sound and practical, but not always palatable.

Reversed Significance

The hard-headed matriarchal streak is overbearing. When this interferes with other people's liberty, trouble is to be expected. The feamle who knows it all is not liked and is soon shunned by one and all. In family circles this trait causes breaks which can never be breached; and in business it results in enmity and opposition.

JACK OF DIAMONDS

The Jack's Significance
This card usually represents a boy or youth, in which case he is seen to have a practical approach to life and will show an affinity for business at an early age. He is highly intelligent. If this card symbolizes an adult, however, immaturity is revealed. Ambition exists but remains unfulfilled because hopes are rarely put into action, either through laziness or a lack of real know-how. He is, however, a potential King. So this individual needs to re-orientate himself if he wants to achieve this status.

Practical Significance
Like the King and Queen of this suit, the Jack is also traditionally seen as fair in appearance. His nature is outward-going, sometimes to the extent of becoming overpoweringly extrovert. He is usually a know-all, but is popular nevertheless because of his *joie de vivre* which results from an endless supply of energy. He does not grow old quickly and retains his youthful appearance to the end.

His opinions are well-known, but only a fool would take his advice seriously. At work he makes an excellent boss's man but lives in hopes of one day making the grade himself. Sexually and socially, he is more of a success because in these circles no one need take him too seriously. Sport is really his line for it offers him the opportunities he craves. Alertness and swiftness may even earn him the vice-captaincy of the local cricket team. In the home his intentions are always good and he is full of promises which he cannot, rather than will not, keep. This is an ambitious, youthful male who is the Jack of all trades when it comes to work.

Psychological Significance
Although he is ambitious, this individual is too immature and unpredictable to ever reach his goal. A little success goes to his head and he is not wise enough to follow it through to the next logical stage. His arrogance is a form of protection, and brooding over the past for too long prevents him from positive forward-planning.

Psychic Significance
As a positive psychic he is often charged with inspiration. However, he should specialize in one of the more mundane occult arts before setting his sights on the higher ranks. He must also be prepared to take orders and obey them, not only for his own safety but for the sake of others, too.

Influential Significance
The personal influence is essentially energetic and youthful even though sound common sense is missing. It is this energy that has helped to keep him going in the absence of real substance. Others may benefit through contact with him by themselves becoming rejuvenated and even inspired. In this sense, this card has a catalystic influence.

Reversed Significance
Stubbornness is his downfall. Unable to believe that he could ever be wrong, his attitude eventually leads to conflict. Untrustworthy and misleading, others may come unstuck through his actions and, in the end, even his charm will let both him and his friends down.

TEN OF DIAMONDS

Numerical Significance

The tenth card of this suit is a sign of completion, indicating that one particular phase in life has ended and another is about to begin. This relates to intellectual and practical aspects: a stage has been reached which is marked by either a change of some sort or an award. It represents a landmark in a career because one goal has been achieved and a step taken on the path to fulfilment. The foundations for future success have been laid.

Practical Significance

A journey which combines business with pleasure will bring a reward. Effort, both physical and mental, is necessary to spark into action a new plan. Past success is not enough, so do not sit and wait too long because a new opportunity is at hand. It is a time for 'off with the old and on with the new' although any loose ends must be firmly tied. Leave no unfinished business before starting on this next new project.

A letter or document will reveal something very important although great care should be exercised in regard to what is committed to paper. A lot of thought is needed to ensure that things start off on the right foot. New buildings or the refurbishing of old ones bring expansion and success, thus laying the foundations for the future.

Life is satisfying on the one hand, but a certain restlessness is felt on the other. This shows it is time to begin something new, or at least to start again on a firmer footing. Plenty of action is symbolized.

Psychological Significance

Extrovert tendencies help increase personal confidence. An active mind needs controlling in order to avoid head-on clashes. Intelligence alone will lead to frustration and a waste of energy.

Psychic Significance

Powerful external forces will be encountered, therefore occult laws must be observed in order to prevent any adverse rebounds. A point of initiation is reached and all who pass this test will gain confidence.

Influential Significance

The influence from this card will produce action although the outcome is not clear at this time. At least it will start things moving. On the practical level, matters will be resolved after an initial period of movement and a certain amount of upheaval. It is time to progress, so new plans should be ready for implementation.

Reversed Significance
A threat of failure will bring hopes and plans crashing to the ground. A lack of direction brings matters to a standstill. Enthusiasm and drive are replaced by anxiety and fear, thus making the future appear decidedly dark.

NINE OF DIAMONDS

Numerical Significance
The ninth card in this suit is a sign of courage resulting from previous stability. It indicates leadership qualities but warns that such a position should not be allowed to go to one's head and produce a tyrannical boss or over-enthusiastic superior, whose ambitions are achieved at the expense of others. The warning is that the higher one climbs, the further one has to fall. Numerically, this warning is borne out because number nine is the last of the single figures which then return to nought in the unit column.

Practical Significance
New interests are to be expected. These are associated with work, ambitions or practical pastimes and may be connected with a journey or travel. A holiday could prove both educational and relaxing, with long-term practical benefits.

Promotion is offered and new business ventures are assured of success. It is time to start building for the future, so lay the foundations as soon as it is practically possible. Opportunities must be taken when they arise because second chances are not on offer. Energy will be forthcoming as a result of hard work, whether mental or physical, so the necessary drive will not be lacking. Individuality must be preserved although a compromise with co-workers is also required. Too much thinking could overshadow the human aspect of a project, thus preventing the final goal from achieving its blue print perfection.

Ideas begin to expand, even to the extent of building castles in the air because, with the courage of true conviction, these too will one day become realities. Extended horizons are indicated.

Psychological Significance
Single-mindedness brings success although this way of thinking needs tempering before it develops into self-righteousness. Stubborn ways prevent full expression.

Psychic Significance
A practical approach to occult matters will bring greater rewards than tackling them from a psychic angle. Positive results can be expected as long as feet are placed firmly on the ground.

Influential Significance
This influence brings confidence and encouragement to the scene. If bold steps have to be taken, these will prove to be easier than anticipated or feared. Practical matters will be resolved best by tackling them in a straightforward way. So be brave and honest in the knowledge that unseen forces are working in your favour.

Reversed Significance
Delays and disagreements hinder the completion of projects and any chance of final success. Lack of courage and self-doubt bring matters pretty well to a standstill. Yet obstinacy prevents a new standpoint from being adopted. Energy is soon dissipated and replaced by a general feeling of disinterest.

EIGHT OF DIAMONDS

Numerical Significance
The eighth card in this suit is a contradiction because it signifies either complete success or utter failure. This is a difficult number: it tends to bring too much of everything and therefore usually amounts to nothing in the end. The ancients saw this as equality and negation, numerically symbolized by the dual proportions two and four. Unfortunately, this make for indecision all round.

The Practical Significance

Short journeys connected with business and the furthering of aims will be undertaken. Minor aspects associated with other practical pursuits, including sport, will be to the fore. A visit away from town brings new ideas as well as providing an opportunity to catch up on things.

If things do not go as well as expected, a trip into the country is advised. Getting away, even briefly, gives one the opportunity to see the situation from a fresh point of view.

This card also indicates that too much thought and effort may have been put into a scheme, so take a temporary break. See this stage as a stepping-stone on the way; but ensure that the next move is forwards and not backwards. Much will depend on personal reactions to circumstances, so stand firm. If in doubt, do not make final decisions, but allow time to be the judge. Much will be revealed with patience. There is still plenty of hope and time for a successful outcome, so regard any delays as a necessary evil. Balance and counterbalance are strongly symbolized.

Psychological Significance

Inner conflict produces muddled thinking. Such confusion may appear to be unending because the mind will continually seek outwards for answers. There is little connection between the conscious and unconscious mind at this time.

Psychic Significance

Positive occult forces will accentuate messages from dogmatic religions. These must be recognized and challenged in order to prevent them from influencing the work in hand.

Influential Significance
This influence is likely to bring stalemate and frustration to a situation. It will be difficult to make a move one way or the other: the answer is to wait rather than to be too hasty. Efforts will not meet with immediate results, no matter how much is put into a scheme. However, in retrospect, nothing will have been wasted.

Reversed Significance
Indecision will lead to complications and lost opportunities. Exhaustion results from allowing energy to be wasted in the wrong directions. Loss of drive brings self-recrimination and others, too, are likely to suffer from a wrong move made in haste. It is, however, never too late to start again.

SEVEN OF DIAMONDS

Numerical Significance
The seventh card in this suit signifies completeness in a practical way. It compares with the collectiveness of the seven colours of the rainbow and the seven notes in the musical scale. Representing that aspect which relates to practical hopes for the future, it includes all materialistic possibilities associated with the external world. It is a positive number offering success, provided that the laws of action and reaction are constantly observed.

Practical Significance
This card represents the individual in relation to the outer world. If practical plans for the future have not already been made, then this should be done immediately. It also urges that such plans should be made as simple and concise as possible, then kept firmly in mind as the goal to be achieved.

Representing the personal driving force, this card is closely linked with ideals and ambitions. Artistic talents and everything connected with stage, screen and television are also included. Communicating with others will be easier from now on so, if you have a special message you wish to communicate, get this across as soon as possible. Public speakers and politicians will find this a good time to go into action and the more effort that is put into a project, the greater the benefit is likely to be.

Life will be seen from a fresh angle and renewed hopes stand a good chance of being fulfilled. Energy levels are high, allowing plenty of physical and mental effort to be applied to schemes and activities. A sporting achievement is on the cards too, because the spirit of ambition means to triumph.

Psychological Significance
'Know thyself' through self-discipline is the message here. Yet it is necessary to balance extrovert tendencies with introvert feelings before a true understanding of the self can be accomplished.

Psychic Significance
The spirit will express itself in a very positive way. It may astrally project to far away places and return with gems of wisdom. Dreams will prove most helpful.

Influential Significance
A strong personal influence emanates from this card. Drive, enthusiasm and strength of purpose are ready and waiting to go into action. This will result in the completion of any unfinished business, as well as the initiation of new projects. Material and practical self-reliance is assured, thus generating further self-confidence.

Reversed Significance
Failing to take opportunities will frustrate and annoy unless the general attitude towards life is altered. Wasted talents and an absence of drive and ambition may be due to lack of vitality. A personal stock-taking is necessary: reassess all practical aspects and plans for the future.

SIX OF DIAMONDS

Numerical Significance
The sixth card in this suit symbolizes possibilities and ambitions

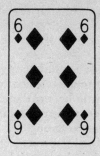

which are often difficult to achieve. Practical plans and material possessions tend to lack real substance even though a lot of hard work has been put into them. This number carries a warning message that one can fall to the ground if caught between two stools, so complete one project before starting on the next one.

Practical Significance

Documents in relation to property, business, work, careers and aims are symbolized by this card. A dispute is likely unless extra care is taken when signing important papers or agreements, so read the small print carefully. On a personal level, refrain from committing to paper anything that could not be repeated in public. Information leaks could cause trouble, as could indiscreet statements made in personal letters.

Much is going on behind the scenes although this may not be apparent at this time. A situation could, therefore, appear to be a paradox. Plans to travel may be upset at the last minute although they will right themselves at the eleventh hour. At work, disagreements due to unforeseen circumstances result in delays although no permanent damage is caused; in the home, differences of opinions arise over practical issues. Relying on the intellect too much produces a one-sided view of a situation. If logic is abandoned, a sudden flash of inspiration should occur to throw light on everything.

Psychological Significance

Material worries weigh heavily and cause tension. Difficulties in accepting the true situation aggravate negative tendencies. So beware of disagreements and bad tempers all round.

Psychic Significance

Beware of instability within a group of positive occultists. This could be due to the absence of negative-receptive psychics who would redress the balance.

Influential Significance
This influence is conveyed mainly through the written word. The pen is mightier than the sword, especially in business matters, so watch out for misconstructions, misleading statements and verbal barbs. Action is necessary to restore stability, therefore this influence should be utilized for this purpose.

Reversed Significance
If allowed to continue, undercover actions will disrupt plans. A lost document or letter will delay the completion of a project and hopes for an early settlement will begin to fade. Be prepared for last minute set-backs owing to the unreliability of others.

FIVE OF DIAMONDS

Numerical Significance
The fifth card in this suit symbolizes mankind, full of practical hopes and potential for the future. From the germ of an idea, it is possible for a far-reaching plan, which has the power to alter one life or many, to develop. This card offers fulfilment, but it is up to the individual to accept or reject the challenge.

Practical Significance
This card holds great promise for the future, providing that opportunities are taken when they arise. There is plenty of originality, but this requires drive to accomplish anything lasting and worth-while. Difficulties may be encountered initially but, once started, the road to success lies ahead.

A move from present property to new or different accommodation is indicated. A journey is in the offing too, providing a change of scenery; this could be a holiday or a business trip. Education and matters associated with the increase of knowledge will come under review, and changes will need to be made in order to get the best results.

Promotions and improvements are there for the asking but, again, it is up to the individual to take the opportunities offered. This is a testing time, but those who are ready and willing to face the challenges will reap the benefits of their hard labours for a long time to come. Personal opportunities which should not be missed are symbolized.

Psychological Significance
Stability of the outward-going aspect of the personality will help achieve extrovert ambitions and goals. This aspect has developed independently from the opposite, introvertive, side, so attention should be paid to the heart as well as the head from now on.

Psychic Significance
The urge to work alone should not be encouraged. Positive psychism within the group will bring safer and surer individual progress as well as results.

Influential Significance
This influence highlights practical failings as well as abilities. It gives an opportunity for one to discover weaknesses and strengths and it is therefore worth-while taking the time to learn in which direction your real talents lie. New plans should be laid on the foundations of past experiences. This will make the most of the positive aspects because these hold out the promise of eventual success.

Reversed Significance
Frustration, due to lack of success, does little to put matters right. If ever perseverance was needed, it is now; so try, try, try again. A journey could cause extra inconvenience, but any action is better than none, so make the best of things and go with the stream, not against it.

FOUR OF DIAMONDS

Numerical Significance

The fourth card in this suit is not an easy card to accept. As it represents the square of two, it adds complications to any situation which already offers two alternatives. If determination and logic are applied, the result will be a firm victory and progress; but if dithering and indecision are allowed to take over, then all semblance of a set plan will disintegrate.

Practical Significance

Whichever way you look at this card, difficult decisions arise. Opposition to even the most carefully prepared plans are inevitable; even last minute alternatives are likely to appear as if from nowhere. These difficult choices are likely to arise in matters relating to jobs, business, new houses, material possessions and holidays: everything, in fact, concerned with the practical side of life. Even letter-writing is likely to pose problems.

Too much consideration of a problem or situation is just as bad as too little, however, because both add up to a null and void. In intellectual circles, contradictions produce anger, mainly because there is more than a grain of truth in the opposing points of view. This disrupts stable beliefs, with the result that insecurity creeps into the situation. This is not the right time to make decisions. It may even be a question of the time of the year because the four seasons have a very powerful effect on all mundane matters. What might be easily accomplished in the heat of the summer is an impossiblity in deep midwinter.

Psychological Significance

Instability is expressed in extrovertive ways and other people notice this. Hang-ups associated with work produce exaggerated character-istics which scare away others, even friends.

Psychic Significance
Occult forces do battle to unbalance the situation. Consant protection and challenging is necessary. When contacting and manipulating these powerful forces, they must not only be guarded against but recognized for what they are and what they can do. To reverse the balance of power, use their mirror image.

Influential Significance
This influence pulls in many directions t once. Loyalties to colleagues, on the one hand, are at loggerheads with what is practically best, on the other. Deals tend to cool off as a result. Communications with others are difficult because of crossed lines. So, when in doubt during this period, do not commit your comments to paper or air them verbally.

Reversed Significance
Fragmented plans and impossible ideas waste time and energy so it would be better to scrap everything and start again. Only by concentrating on one aspect at a time will any real progress be made. There is a lack of co-ordination between hopes and the implementa-tion of them: a stalemate situation exists.

THREE OF DIAMONDS

Numerical Significance
The third card in this suit has a built-in stability which can provide help for practical aims and ambitions. It is a good sign, indicating that now is the time to take a step forward because your plans are

based on firm foundation. Creativity should blossom from this point and as this card signifies a source of knowledge, further original ideas can be expected. Confidence in practical ability encourages the expansion and development on all fronts relating to business, hobbies, pleasure and leisure.

Practical Significance

Plans for the future are on a firm footing, but determination to see these through to a successful conclusion will be necessary. If this is lacking, even the best laid schemes can founder, so focus your attention on the final objective and keep this in view all the time.

Energy is available for physical and mental work, so utilize this without delay. Original ideas are waiting to be recognized and, when they are, they should be applied to any old projects which require new stimulus. Academic theses, symbolized by the Cambridge tripos exams, are represented by this card. Thus, intellectual work will suddenly become easier as the barrier to knowledge is pushed back. This is a good time to think about exams and tests because any results from these should be excellent.

Ingenuity, originality and determination make ideal partners in the practical and intellectual fields of life, so it is not surprising that this card symbolizes a blend of past, present and future hopes.

Psychological Significance

Positivity produces a very determined and outwardly stable person. Too much determination could develop into selfishness, however. So, if you do not wish to appear to be on an ego trip, match this determination with thought for others.

Psychic Significance

Harmonious relationships with psychic co-workers and positive occult forces will bring great spiritual rewards. Help and healing directed now will give good results.

Influential Significance

Should lack of enthusiasm slow down practical, material or intellectual progress, then this influence will introduce determination onto the scene. As a result, positivity and drive return, bringing the end object within grasp. Hard work is still necessary, but with this incentive it will seem much easier to achieve positive results. A form of isolation could be experienced as the result of utilizing this determination, but a 'go-it-alone' course is likely to prove far more rewarding than one which is dependent on the whim of others: the prize does not have to be shared, for one thing!

Reversed Significance
Owing to laziness or lack of drive, a distinct difficulty will be encountered in the achievement of a hope, ambition or project. A plan is desperately needed to escape from the present circumstances which are static and frustrating. Physical efforts are liable to be wasted as things now stand, so try to take stock of the situation.

TWO OF DIAMONDS

Numerical Significance
The second card in this suit is a paradox. Two practical aspects have to be considered and united into a whole, if at all possible. Two heads are better than one – except when they disagree with each other. All or nothing situations develop and the introduction of an alternative is bound to throw something out of balance temporarily.

Practical Significance
This card offers partnerships and delicately balanced relationships between two people linked through business, practical working arrangements or the domestic side of marriage. Both should contribute to the whole by using their individual experiences to bring about a productive joint situation. When the aim is the same, harmony exists; but if one party loses sight of this objective, disharmony will result.

It is difficult to keep a balance all the time because duality tends to make final decisions very difficult; and knowing there is a choice only make things worse. Communication between partners could lead to trouble too, because meanings are not conveyed properly, so extra care must be taken when expressing a point.

If progress with plans slows down, take one step at a time. Good ideas are lacking because parallel lines can never meet – seek out the balanced way. Great tact will be necessary in order to prevent a permanent rift, yet if the right cards are played, agreement and unification will eventually result.

Psychological Significance
Split intentions divide attention on the practical front. Thoughts tend to run in parallel lines which never converge. Energy is wasted, so tiredness is to be expected.

Psychic Significance
Difficulties with two positive aspects confuse occultists. It is easy to go down the wrong psychic track so be careful to challenge all forces in use.

Influential Significance
This influence brings duality which will not always help a current situation. Since this has the effect of introducing a choice or alternative solution it is only later that its true value will be seen and appreciated. Indecision is the worst aspect but, on the other hand, it is important to ensure that the other side of the coin is not forgotten either. The reward from this lies in the future, not the present.

Reversed Significance
Ambitions will be overshadowed by obstacles and practical difficulties. Opposition to a plan makes matters seem impossible and any amount of hard work will have little or no effect. An all or nothing situation has developed, with the result that there is the possibility of falling between two stools.

CLUBS

ACE OF CLUBS

Numerical Significance
This is the first and last card in the suit. It combines the numbers one and thirteen which, together, form a pool of wealth. This gives stability and security to individuals as well as firing them with the enthusiasm necessary to search for that proverbial pot of gold at the end of the rainbow. This card is a power in itself and needs careful handling but, if used with discretion and understanding, it attracts all the good things in life. On one level it brings materialistic prizes and, on another, the wealthy reward of wisdom.

Practical Significance
Good fortune lies in this card. Wealth is on the horizon and is well within the questioner's grasp. Speculation has paid off handsomely, bringing material comforts and plenty of worldly goods. There is a warning though; remember the saying: 'Easy come, easy go' because this is a possibility. Permanence is not a special feature of this card, so watch interests carefully.

The way in which such financial wealth is used is most important. If rewarded as one of the talents it will bring help and happiness to many people. So, casting bread on the waters of life can result in rich rewards for everyone. Those who have used personal ability to attain high standards in life will be rewarded with national or even international fame. Industrious folk will reach their goal through inventiveness and devotion, whilst others may well inherit money or titled status.

At one end of the scale this card can signify a big pools win, a legacy or a generous gift; whilst at the other, it represents recognition as a star performer, politician or actor.

Psychological Significance
A strong desire to possess objects of material value overshadows the simple things in life. You should allow those underlying characteristics which lie nearer to your heart to express themselves.

Psychic Significance
A special psychic gift will come to light. If this is used according to occult law, a great wealth of understanding will add to an ever-deepening pool of wisdom.

Influential Significance
The influence from this card instantly helps flagging financial resources. It brings respite from money worries and allows the individual time to reorganize his or her affairs. Although this may not solve the problem, it will certainly give an opportunity to recuperate funds. Speculation and a new approach to wealth will develop, so use this influence to attain a particular goal or standard.

Reversed Significance
Dependence on money for security and pleasures in life will soon reveal the lack of substance such a pursuit brings. Dis-satisfaction, linked to an inability to alter course, produces frustration and poverty of pocket and outlook.

KING OF CLUBS

The King's Significance
This King is the experienced man, crowned with financial success. A stockpile of worldly goods allows time in later life to pursue wealth on a higher plane. Self-confidence arises mainly from material assets, but opportunities will arise later which should put this on a more intuitive footing. Imagination is not lacking, but if this is

directed one way only, it will lead to limitations. A collector of most things – from valuable antiques to a load of old rubbish – this King is seen to be a very single-minded person, with an eye for making a quick profit.

Practical Significance

Traditionally, this is one of the dark, rich-complexioned kings, full of life, sexual vitality and good ideas. Many seek his advice, mainly because he appears to have done so well for himself. Although he is completely trustworthy as far as his intentions go, he may lack sufficient experience to be considered an expert.

Tycoons and financiers are represented by this card and, very often, it is their single-mindedness that has brought them to the peak of their success rather than careful, intelligent planning. Ruthlessness possesses such individuals when they are on this road to success because they know that if they weaken or are deflected off course, they stand to lose.

When this king is the big fish in a little pond, everyone knows it. Modesty is not among his attributes and being in demand is one of his greatest pleasures. Acting as the kingpin suits him and he guards his territory jealously; those who take liberties are castigated, but those who come with cap in hand are more than welcome. In this attitude, shades of insecurity can be seen and this trait is found in even the richest of financial wizards.

Psychological Significance

This king possesses the good quality of perseverence. This attribute should be used with discretion, however, or it might be mistaken for over-forcefulness. He has a rich pool of experience from which to draw but, again, care has to be taken or he could appear boastful.

Psychic Significance
Even though he is an experienced psychic, he still seeks proof that other dimensions really exist. Until he can accept these instinctively and intuitively he will remain at his present stage of initiation.

Influential Significance
This gives control over finances and wealth generally, so influential help with any monetary problems can be expected. This may come from an experienced person qualified in banking or from a changed situation. Loans, if needed, arise from reliable sources and, although expensive, will restore that lost security. A fortunate gift of money or a useful present will brighten life temporarily but, for permanence, this card's influence should be utilized to put personal affairs in order.

Reversed Significance
Miserliness produces a narrow mind that shuts out the true meaning of life. Greed, deception and covetous ways eventually lead to loneliness. The individual's inability to accept changes results in personal limitation and, unless care is exercised, leads to a hermit's life. Fear of losing what has been hoarded encourages false suspicions to develop, so that family as well as friends stay away from the door.

QUEEN OF CLUBS

The Queen's Significance
This Queen is the feminine aspect of the suit. She is an efficient, successful woman who is used to plenty of money and knows what it can buy. Material luxuries often become a necessity so that when times are hard and these are lacking, she becomes unsociable and bad tempered. As a business woman she has her own interests at

heart, rather than those of clients or customers and can, therefore, be regarded as somewhat self-centred. A rich husband is often her source of wealth but, when needs be, she had a good head for making money.

Practical Significance

Traditionally, this queen represents a dark-haired, richly complexioned woman. Active and generous, she enjoys charitable work and organizing others into action. She often acts the lady bountiful, expecting compliments and admiration for her efforts. Wealth, her prop and support, will occasionally be used to promote others, but they are expected to show her endless gratitude in return.

These characteristics show up more and more with increasing years yet, should she find herself alone, she is well able to look after herself and become the bread-winner. Her place, she feels, is in the home but not around the kitchen sink; so any opportunity to go out is seized upon immediately. Lavish in most respects, she is always well and fashionably dressed. Most men admire her cool, sophisticated appearance, but few realize just how expensive she can be until it is too late!

Vitality gives this queen an attraction which makes her the envy of other women, who tend to be jealous of her. This is probably why deep friendships are virtually non-existent. In sports she finds the perfect setting to prove and show herself off; usually, she excels in these and wins many prizes.

Psychological Significance

This woman is an independent thinker, a characteristic which has its benefits although loneliness may develop later through lack of proper communication with others. Her need to possess material objects shows that she looks outwards for security instead of inwards, where personal reserves wait to be recognized and tapped.

Psychic Significance

Occult work is carried out positively and negatively. This brings a wealth of experience but also highlights personal psychic strengths and weakness.

Influential Significance

Personal self-confidence will receive a powerful boost from this positive influence. A temporary self-centredness may develop, but this is just what is required at this time. The effects are generally uplifting, so you can expect an increase in wealth which acts as a safeguard against impending trouble as well as allowing you the time to think and replan for the future.

Reversed Significance
This represents a mean, bad tempered and suspicious woman who cannot keep a friend for long. Always greedy for more and wanting to keep up with the Jones's, she becomes inquisitive and prying, with a result that more doors close than will ever be opened. She is her own worst enemy.

JACK OF CLUBS

The Jack's Significance
When representing a boy or youth this card shows that there is a strong desire to reach the heights and become head boy, captain of the cricket team or the organizer of interests other than the three Rs. Although not an academic, he is a budding tycoon because he has the ability to accumulate wealth and fortune.

If representing an adult, this card represents one who is stuck on the treadmill of life. The result is that this individual never hits the jackpot which was once well within his range.

Practical Significance
Full of vitality, he enjoys taking on responsibility at an early age. Able to save money, he soon learns the advantages that a nest-egg provides; therefore his talents turn automatically towards hoarding more and more. He will always make a determined effort to keep a bargain, although his personal aim or ambition will always be first and foremost in his mind. It is often said that he has an old head on young shoulders yet to put implicit trust in him would be most unwise.

Experience is what is needed and this, combined with the exuberance of youth, holds out great possibilities. To achieve kingly status he must beware of the trap which would keep him at his present knavely level for the rest of his life. How successful he is in this aim will depend on how adventurous he is when opportunities arise.

A degree of risk is involved in making the grade, so chances must be taken if true aims and ambitions are ever to be achieved. This Jack is the only one who can afford to take such chances and get away with it.

Psychological Significance
This character finds difficulty in keeping to one thing at a time. Hopefulness makes up for this defect and carries him through to a limited success. He has the ability to see ahead but does not always rely on his own judgment. Other people let him down yet he does not seem to learn his lesson.

Psychic Significance
Seeking answers to profound occult problems will prevent steady psychic progress. Don't expect too much too soon or a sharp encounter with a restraining occult force will bring a quick realization of your folly.

Influential Significance
This influence will help boost resources and thus restore faith in oneself. It may manifest as a loyal supporter or as a financial improvement. A racy atmosphere will help to relax any previous tension, so be bold and take a chance on a project, idea or hope. Back hunches to the full because this opportunity may not be repeated for some time.

Reversed Significance
Over-enthusiastic drive produces a dicey character who is regarded as potentially dangerous. The higher he climbs, the further he has to fall and, unfortunately, a fall is on the cards through his own stupidity.

TEN OF CLUBS

Numerical Significance
The tenth card in this suit indicates the completion of one phase and

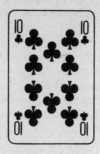

the beginning of the next. The perfection of this number, the first of the multiple numbers, can be compared to the wheel of fate and fortune. Wealth – on all levels – has been accumulated in the last cycle and the future already rests on a secure footing. The phase ahead offers opportunities which, if taken, will provide further increases.

Practical Significance
A welcome sum of money is on the horizon, possibly from an unexpected source. This may materialize in the form of an inheritance, gift or a big gambling win. Security results, thus generating feelings of confidence and anticipation. But be prepared for surprise complications which could temporarily delay the actual arrival of this money.

Much revolves around investments and assets – from the largest fortunes down to post-office savings – so do not let these lie idle for too long. Like the talents in the parable, these will repay you best by being made to work.

This is a good time to spend money on investments for the future, so now is the time to give serious consideration to ways of doing this. Do not sit back and take it easy at this stage or rely too much on past glories. Drive and action is essential to keep the wheel of fate and fortune turning.

Psychological Significance
Hopes will be recharged with energy through personal effort. Fears and doubts are left behind as a new cycle in life begins. Forget the past and look ahead to better times.

Psychic Significance
A gift from the gods helps psychic progress. Philosophically, this

represents the harvesting of a previous sowing: good actions have been followed by good reactions. A new level of awareness is achieved.

Influential Significance
This is a strong, positive, monetary influence which will bring security and confidence to a particular situation. Expect financial matters to stabilize and then steadily improve. Much strength and comfort is given by this material asset and although it is meant to be used, do so only after very careful consideration. Try to insure against future expenditure by acting now. An opportunity to do this will arise shortly.

Reversed Significance
It is virtually impossible to alter present spendthrift habits and, as a result, the last of personal savings ebb and unpaid bills mount up. Without money to act as a form of security, incentive is missing and this keeps the doors of opportunity closed.

NINE OF CLUBS

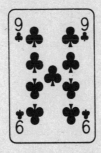

Numerical Significance
The ninth card in this suit is very fortuitous because it attracts further stability in the form of wealth, in every sense of the word. A peak in financial affairs will be reached shortly and this will bring respite from worries. Also, a milestone has been reached, which puts things on a much firmer footing all round. However, this does not mean that it is a foregone conclusion that the future is going to be rich, without any effort being made. In order to maintain this stability, efforts will be needed and now is the time to make plans for this.

Practical Significance

Wealth is definately on the cards. Bank balances will soon look much healthier, possibly due to inheritances, gifts or money from property. Any money owing will also be repaid. One-man businesses will benefit financially, offering the opportunity for further expansion. Material comforts and a lessening of pressure will follow.

Money connected with marriage and close friendships is closely associated with this card. Over-all richness is indicated, but partnerships will need constant attention in order to continue to function as profitable propositions. Marriage settlements following divorce or separation are to the fore and any uncertainty concerning money will end soon. This is the right time to complete outstanding financial arrangements, even if the sum involved is small. Once this is done, freedom from worry follows – and this is a gift in itself.

A prosperous marriage is also indicated although this does not necessarily signify pounds in the bank. A wealth of happiness and mutual understanding accumulates, too. Count your blessings now and they will become a good investment for the future.

Psychological Significance

Confidence reaches a peak. Negativity vanishes, albeit temporarily, so make the most of this opportunity. Good relationships in the home and at work produce a relaxed and happy atmosphere, resulting in peace of mind.

Psuchic Significance

Positive and negative psychism blend and harmonize, thus opening up even more doors on the occult scene. A wealth of new experiences are offered and confidence in one's own ability increases.

Influential Significance

Decisions will be influenced by money. As a deciding factor, finances rather than emotions should be used as the yardstick. Joint savings will produce unexpectedly good results. This influence has a stabilizing effect too, and although things may appear to slow down it is only temporary. This will give you a valuable opportunity to catch up before moving on to the next phase.

Reversed Significance

Present financial stability cannot last much longer. Expenses will increase enormously and quickly outweight income, so expect high personal inflation. Steps should be taken now to prevent a landslide into poverty.

EIGHT OF CLUBS

Numerical Significance

The eighth card in this suit strongly suggests a balance of payments. Riches, on all levels, are difficult to assess at this stage and can be compared with a half full or half empty glass of water: it all depends on the individual standpoint. A rest may be safely taken at this time before starting on the next phase. There is a danger of covering the same ground again by repeating the past, but there should be no turning or looking back, only forward.

Practical Significance

This is the gambler's lucky card. The desire for money and wealth is strong although, at this point, there does not appear to be a watertight plan to bring this about. The solution offered is to take a risk because this is the chance card. Bypass the usual channels and jump in at the deep end, knowing that you stand a very good chance of winning.

On the basic level, play your hunches because inspired guesses about which dog or horse will come in first can be relied upon. Gambling with property and investments, where financial rewards are high, are good bets too. Those not given to risking their shirts should at least be adventurous when investing, buying or selling.

This is a 'nothing ventured nothing gained' situation and unless a positive move is made now, progress will be circular, so beware of arriving back where you started. A bottle-neck has been reached, indicating that the past must be completely settled before turning to the future.

Psychological Significance

Difficulties in understanding personal motives cause worry. Too much self-analysis will only lead to confusion and further complications however, so accept yourself and others for what they are.

Psychic Significance
Powerful influences could easily divert good intentions into the wrong channel. Beware of false values and false prophets who unbalance normally stable psychic atmospheres.

Influential Significance
This influence brings out latent gambling instincts and the desire or necessity for more money will develop. This trend will force some form of action to be taken. Opportunities will arise and these should not be ignored or missed because they can save a lot of time and effort by allowing you to take a short cut to the jackpot.

Reversed Significance
By repeating past mistakes more financial losses will be incurred. A negative vicious circle traps the unwary, with the result that it will become impossible to escape even further losses.

SEVEN OF CLUBS

Numerical Significance
The seventh card in this suit signifies personal success in life and offers security and insurance against the future. Carefully planned efforts have paid off and produced a nest-egg of considerable size. On other levels, too, wealth has accumulated and this may be used profitably in many different ways.

Practical Significance
This card represents the natural ability to make money and attain

materialistic goals. Involvement with financial matters at this time is likely and if the right cards are played, success is ensured. Ambitions and plans concerned with making money, or even a modest living, need to be constantly watched. Past experience shows that this will pay off, so don't let go of the reins now or the initiative will be lost as a result.

Since wealth is comparative, individual situations must be seen in relation to personal circumstances and standpoints: £1 seems a lot to some people but nothing to others. Special care must be taken when dealing with other people's money in order to safeguard personal reputations. Honest intentions are not enough: indicate on paper exactly where the money was spent.

Financial success is definitely on the cards, but due more to personal effort than to good luck. However, ensure that your values do not alter and do not make money into a god.

Psychological Significance
Freedom of self-expression should be encouraged now, using the wealth of past experiences to do so. A mature outlook has developed and should be of great help in solving life's problems.

Psychic Significance
Individual psychic development takes a big step forward. After an exciting phase, doors will open on new dimensions. The value of controlled astral travel will result in an important initiation.

Influential Significance
Personal financial matters will improve considerably with the help of this influence. Businesses benefit too and the domestic front will remain in funds despite heavy outlays. New ideas on how to budget and increase income will develop and this will, in turn, bring the security which has often been lacking in the past.

Reversed Significance
Total disregard for simple accounting brings personal financial troubles. Heavy debts will eventually lead to serious circumstances that could involve others who are in no way to blame. The days of borrowing are past.

SIX OF CLUBS

Numerical Significance

The Sixth card in this sit offers a choice of ways in which to make money and obtain wealth but is not a solution in itself. Much hard work and plodding effort are necessary to bring things together, which will be essential before a move forward can be made with any degree of confidence. Pressure and tension are inevitable, yet these will produce the driving force necessary to start to pull things into shape.

Practical Significance

Help will come from a most unexpected source. This could signify a fortunate turn of events or may indicate that a reliable friend will offer profitable advice. Another possibility is that a loan of hard cash could materialize. So, one way or another, some form of enrichment can be confidently expected.

Income and expenditure will just about remain on an even keel. There is nothing to spare, however, and since there is nothing to cover an emergency either, strict economy measures must be implemented at once. This is not a permanent situation but any action taken now will have good repercussions in the future. Careful planning is all-important, so don't be tempted into rash spending or investing in dicey holdings.

Reliable advice is worth seeking before parting with cash, and such help will be found easily although it may not come from a conventional source. Use instinct along with intellect to forge ahead: using both together will allow a more balanced assessment to be made. Everything must ultimately be paid for in one way or another, so do not forget to make provisions for this.

Psychological Significance
Doubts and fears should be seen in perspective or they will upset balanced judgment. Keep negativity under control by replacing dependence on others by self-reliance.

Psychic Significance
Expect occult influences to manifest in strange ways. Personal coincidences will initiate a new train of thought which will lead to new psychic pastures. Psychic development progresses slowly but surely.

Influential Significance
A helpful influence from out of the blue saves the day. Projects and plans relating to business and family matters which depend on money will benefit greatly. Last minute rescue measures will turn up trumps with the result that disappointment will be avoided and good friends will prove themselves to be as good as their word. Faith is restored all round.

Reversed Significance
There is a tendency to underestimate and overspend. An 'easy come, easy go' attitude may work for a while but, once the scales have been allowed to tip too far in the wrong direction, poverty is on the cards. Such conditions are self-imposed although this does nothing to stop the negative, downhill slide.

FIVE OF CLUBS

Numerical Significance
The fifth card in this suit denotes hopes for a better future. With drive and initative, plus plenty of inspired guesses, it is possible to

work up from nothing to a richly endowed position in life. This could result through an accumulation of material assets or, alternatively, through a wealth of experience. The end objective is quite clear although the road to this success has yet to be fully laid. Taking a new track altogether could provide a solution.

Practical Significance

Money associated with marriage and partnerships is indicated. This may take the form of sharing gifts and inheritances or the taking of rewards from joint business efforts. If equality is absent, a financial arrangement may leave one partner hard up, however, so changes might be necessary. Even though this might mean starting from virtually nothing, it will be worth all the hard work in the end.

Seen as a challenge, an opportunity will present itself which will bring better returns than a previous investment. There is nothing to stop progress once a firm plan is made and, should money troubles develop, they will soon vanish because, once started on that positive road leading towards the end objective, cash will begin to materialize.

Long-term monetary plans, including pension schemes and insurance policies, should be considered now. With an eye on the future – looking especially in the direction of old age – it pays to ensure that the nest will always remain well feathered.

Psychological Significance

Difficulties in dealing with others could become a worry. Weakness of character can lead to mental oppression, so it is important to recognize this tendency before it is too late. To keep the peace is one thing, but to be overpowered is another.

Psychic Significance

Positive psychic protection is necessary when controlling occult forces which are stronger than is realized. Harmony within the group will help to develop this, but if harmony is lacking, unwanted influences will creep into the situation and cause havoc.

Influential Significance

This influence will have long-term effects on wealth generally. At least this will settle things one way or the other and reveal the true financial state, down to the last penny. This can be regarded as a definite starting point, so loook ahead and make those much needed plans for the future. This card holds out great promise that things will go well, provided that personal dedication is applied positively.

Reversed Significance
Lack of initiative in the past continues into the future and there is
little hope of any opportunity, however good, being taken now.
Financially broke, friends are thin on the ground. Devious means of
recouping losses will not provide a solution, however, so such
thoughts should be squashed.

FOUR OF CLUBS

Numerical Significance
The fourth card in this suit indicates a struggle to keep things on an
even keel. Resources could be drained in several directions at once,
leaving little in reserve. However, if a half is called now, a firm basis is
left, upon which a secure, four square future could be built. If
arrangements involve partners, special care must be taken to
maintain the necessary harmony and balance or all could be lost
completely.

Practical Significance
There is a strong warning in this card concerning the loss of a
valuable article. Extra precautions should be taken to ensure that
material possessions such as keys, jewellery, purses or gloves as well
as cash, cars or furniture are not stolen or lost. The call on financial
reserves could be a lot heavier than anticipated and limitations
imposed as a result. The solution lies in keeping well within the
bounds of solvency.

A loss of faith in oneself leads to lack of self-confidence and to lack
of trust in others who have, in the past, been most reliable. This can
cause insecurity, so keep the question of balance in mind when
trying to regain equilibrium. Equal but opposing forces will either
negate or destroy each other or harmonize into a positive force

which can help to stabilize the situation.

Psychological Significance
Inhibitions seek outlets and, in so doing, may appear as extreme behaviour. Mental highs and lows produce mood swings, but this is only a temporary stage and will pass. Try to steer a middle course, especially when in the presence of others.

Psychic Significance
There is a risk that too much psychic work will drain off too much energy. This will not help anyone, so take a rest from occult encounters in order to keep at least one foot on the ground.

Influential Significance
Demands from several directions at once produce an influence that draws heavily upon resources. So, expect savings to dwindle and, on a physical level, be prepared for energy to drain away. Since it is difficult to do much about things at present, it is best to sit tight, relax and wait for a change of atmosphere.

Reversed Significance
Extreme difficulties will be encountered regarding money matters. Distrust of everyone and everything brings negotiations to a halt and produces an infuriating stalemate. Snap decisions will invariably be wrong, so do nothing rather than make more mistakes.

THREE OF CLUBS

Numerical Significance
The third card in this suit offers stability in respect of resources. Acting as a reservoir from which to draw, businesses will recover and

thrive, and the launching of new projects will prove remarkably easy. Enthusiasm fires ambitions into action and things will grow from this point into profitable reality. Those who have experienced failure in the past should try again, for the time is now right to make another attempt.

Practical Significance
Financial stability gives the materialistic self-assurance which has been lacking until now. Progress in all directions is on the cards, although opportunities still need to be recognized and grasped before they will pay off. There will be good co-operation between partners and this, plus firm financial backing, signifies that plans, schemes and proposals stand every chance of success.

A stage has been reached where new and profitable ideas will emerge on many levels. In a mundane respect, financial benefits from an expanding business can be expected. From a personal standpoint, valuable past experiences will be put into action to form a source of wealth from which to draw when in trouble and in need of strength of purpose.

Individual potential invested in business, artistic pursuits or on the domestic front now will express itself in very rewarding ways. Excellent foundations exist on which to build for the future, and now is the time to do this with every confidence. There is more than a grain of truth in the saying 'third time lucky', so prove this right by acting on intuition backed up by experience.

Psychological Significance
Reserves are high, bringing mental stability and confidence in oneself. Unification of ideas will blend into a new creative stream of thought, leading to future fulfilment.

Psychic Significance
The occult 'law of three requests' is encountered. When challenging entities and forces, use this law in order to be absolutely certain of their true identity.

Influential Significance
This is a stabilizing influence which gives confidence and introduces security into schemes and projects. Money matters will begin to look a lot healthier soon and will continue to improve for some time. A prosperous atmosphere shines on the domestic front, so extravagances are excusable just now.

Reversed Significance
Self-reproach for wasted opportunities leads to aggression and anger. As hopes fade, they are replaced with despair but, since no effort is made to really alter, this must be expected.

TWO OF CLUBS

Numerical Significance
The second card in this suit indicates a duality which is likely to produce head-on clashes and opposition associated with wealth and its distribution. Discussions with partners or financial advisers appear to offer no solution, yet, at the same time, efforts must be made because nothing ventured means nothing gained. Eventually, the balance will be restored, but keep an eye on both sides of the fence until this happens.

Practical Significance
A change of circumstances brings uncertainty but this is inevitable. In practical terms, money matters prove worrying although real fears for the future are quite unfounded. The joining of forces is one answer to the problem but, since this is not yet possible, it is better to go it alone.

Although joint efforts may appear to halve responsibilities and liabilities, they could, at the same time, double mental strain through such an arrangement. One aspect has, therefore, to be weighed against the other. On the whole, any pressure to pool resources should be resisted in the knowledge that a lone effort will more than double rewards.

The reckless spending of money or energy will not be recouped easily, so this is not the time for action generally. Projects launched now have only a fifty-fifty chance of success; therefore, it is better to wait for a sign that leaves no doubt whatsoever that the time is right and the door wide open.

Psychological Significance
The conscious and unconscious minds form a link which increases awareness and understanding of oneself and others. Care must be exercised, however, in order to maintain a good balance between the emotions and the intellect. Further development of the character will grow naturally from this duality as long as a careful balance is maintained.

Psychic Significance
Working as both a positive and negative psychic will increase the individual's powers tremendously and result in a greater degree of responsibility. A good, balanced philosophy of selflessness and compassion is very necessary therefore because the welfare and safety of others is at stake.

Influential Significance
Although this is an opposing influence it often does a lot more good than harm in the end because it lessens the urge to spend unwisely on non-essentials. The twin nature of this card inhibits positive decisions, yet, again, this acts as a brake just at the right time and thus protects resources. Do not throw caution to the winds however, but stand with both feet firmly on the ground in readiness for the next phase.

Reversed Significance
Opposition destroys every vestige of hope and kills enthusiasm. Vindictive partners inhibit self-expression and make life thoroughly miserable. Double the price has to be paid for innocent mistakes.

HEARTS

ACE OF HEARTS

Numerical Significance
This is the first and last card in the suit: a combination which produces fulfilment and wisdom. Nourishment to feel and sustain all heartfelt desires stems from this and happiness is initiated too, which affects all emotional situations. New friendships and reunions are activated, offering lasting friendship and love in the future. As a source of energy, this manifests on many levels, beginning with sexual and physical attractions and going on to compassionate feelings for humanity and all living creatures as a whole.

Practical Significance
Everything the heart desires is in this card. A happy family, true friends, passionate lovers and continued peace of mind are all definite possibilities. Heartfelt hopes and wishes stand a very good chance of being realized because fate and fortune shine benignly on the happiness scene at this time.

A surge of benevolent energy from this source of plenty rejuvenates and heals tired bodies and minds. Having received this, kindly feelings and thoughts for others are generated which, in turn, reward the individual with a satisfying, inner harmony.

Socially, opportunities arise which offer the chance of meeting many new friends and those in search of a lover will find themselves in the right place at the right time. Romantic settings materialize in the most unexpected places and relationships blossom speedily in this atmosphere. Sex and excitement soon enter the scene and these are followed, more often than not, by long-standing arrangements. Fertility is also symbolized by this card, so the beginnings of a new family circle could follow suit and the whole cycle of life begin once again.

Psychological Significance
Strong emotions need to be controlled because the heart definitely rules the head at this time. Judgment could well be very unbalanced from this singular standpoint although a good balance should develop eventually, once it is realized that a one-sided outlook exists.

Psychic Significance
A pool of compassion and understanding is ready and waiting to be tapped by those who wish to do so. Healing energy arises from this source and may be utilized for self-healing or directed towards others who need it. This force pours oil on troubled waters and protects the innocent.

Influential Significance
This is a strong, compassionate influence which can be used in any situation that lacks love and understanding. It will calm down the irate, bring balance to an over-materialistic situation and, by introducing humour into a worrying monetary problem, remove fears completely. Purely in its own right, this card has the power to introduce emotional happiness and inner satisfaction.

Reversed Significance
A barren situation is to be expected. Lack of understanding, absence of feeling for others and a general bleakness dispels all hope of emotional happiness. A big disappointment results in loneliness – with a broken heart hiding beneath a shattered exterior.

KING OF HEARTS

The King's Significance
This King is the great lover of the pack. He expresses himself with deep feelings coloured by the dictates from his heart. His ambition is to collect plenty of admirers and notch up sexual conquests but, with the increasing years, he turns more towards philosophical concepts. In many ways, he is a self-centred person and cannot see himself as he really is. He sincerely believes his heart is in the right place and that this is enough.

Practical Significance
Traditionally, this King is a fair-haired, blue-eyed man who is very emotional and thinks mainly with his heart. Above all, he is a great lover. This makes him a warn-hearted person who is friendly, kind, generous, well liked and popular. He is the home-loving type and therefore puts this side of life before his career and materialistic ambitions. As a father he plays for hours with the children.

Since he is an incurable romantic, he attracts the opposite sex and takes them in completely. Flattery and compliments pour from him and he has the gift of bestowing himself on one woman at a time, creating the impression that she is the only person in the world so far as he is concerned. Inwardly though, he is really a loner who exists in a secret place surrounded by his own thoughts. Others rarely know him although they often think they do.

His artistic nature can be channelled into various directions and, in the home, often manifests as a pretty garden and, at work, as a tidy desk. This neatness makes up for his apparent lack of originality although this trait is not lacking when it comes to pursuits nearer to his loving heart.

Psychological Significance

Heartfelt emotions nearly always hold sway over reason and logic. He has a great need to love and be loved, compassionately as well as sexually. There is a danger, however, that this individual will become withdrawn as he grows older.

Psychic Significance

Strong receptive qualities show good mediumistic ability which, when partnered by positive psychic communications, will extend well into the 'great unknown'. This King may also represent masculine discarnate beings such as departed fathers, uncles or grandfathers.

Influential Significance

This is the loving influence, whether from a lover, parent or good friend. It has the power to persuade and charm the birds off the trees, if necessary. Sometimes glib words accompany it and are accepted as pearls of wisdom, but only time will tell if these are true or false. Advice flows freely from the heart although, since this is based on emotions not on sound, practical experience, it cannot really be taken too seriously.

Reversed Significance

A tendency towards selfish sexual gratification does nothing to fulfil the desires in the long run. This attitude may attract a wide circle of off-beat acquaintances, yet such company will only end up by being despised thoroughly.

QUEEN OF HEARTS

The Queen's Significance

When young, this character represents the lover, and the blushing bride. As she grows older, she becomes the comfortable little woman in the home whose limited outlook extends little further than the end of the garden. She tends to develop interests which focus solely around the kitchen sink, and a bit of gossip. Ambitions are at a minimum beyond this point, yet contentment seems to grow rather than diminish with time.

Practical Significance

This Queen is generally regarded as a fair-haired person, yet this exterior, like the superficial image of all the court cards, is unreliable. When a girl, her hopes dwell on an early marriage, a home of her own and a family.

Potentially a ready-made mother, a good friend to the neighbours and a thoroughly domesticated person, she asks for no more than peace and quiet in the home. Romantic notions make her the queen of the kitchen where she takes pride in cooking, cleaning and everything within the scope of the domestic scene. Once married, however, her standpoint changes. She drops the glamour – which once lured every male in sight – for a stouter, almost dowdy image of the mistress of the house.

Artistic talents grow with middle-aged spread and what emerges usually surprises everyone: pretty paintings and romantic story-writing were invented for the typical Queen of Hearts.

Emotions are slowly conquered over the years and self-assurance grows from inner self-satisfaction rather than from intellectual confidence.

Psychological Significance

Seeing life from an emotional point of view gives a very one-sided picture. This leads to over-sensitivity and, eventually, to self-pity. Introversion should be counteracted by more outside interests in order to restore the balance as soon as possible.

Psychic Significance

This Queen is a natural medium. It is important that she learns to control this gift properly, however, before uninvited influences intrude and take over. Good protection is essential, therefore. This card may also represent feminine discarnate beings, such as departed mothers, aunts or grandmothers.

Influential Significance
This influence offers good motherly advice. Compassion and a reliable shoulder to cry on help to release tension, particularly as confidences will be respected. A friendly atmosphere restores harmony both inside and outside the home and, generally, happiness reigns.

Reversed Significance
A self-centred outlook limits a fertile imagination and this eventually frustrates and demoralizes a normally placid nature. Friends become few and far between and interests diminish. Day dreams replace practical plans and further obstacles prevent emotional happiness. Dreariness overshadows the domestic scene.

JACK OF HEARTS

The Jack's Significance
As a boy or young man this knave is full of fun. If he matures emotionally he will become the King of Hearts, yet he will always retain that boyish look throughout his life. Potentially a kind person, he seems to miss out when it comes to hand outs and experiences difficulties in being taken seriously. This causes frustration. A general aura of immaturity – a characteristic which, once recognized, is never forgotten – makes him the symbolic Peter Pan.

Practical Significance
He is, like the King and Queen of this suit, traditionally fair. Easygoing all his life, he enjoys sport more for the sociability it offers than for the exercise. Although a competitive spirit is lacking, a sporting attitude to life is not – so he is very popular, especially with the ladies. At work, promotion seems to pass him by, but since happiness and

an easy-going life are his chief aims, this does not bother him unduly.

When in love he can be hurt easily and shows it, too. His habit of wearing his heart on his sleeve does not help in this respect and he is prone to make unfortunate relationships anyway. When married, he is often thought to be his wife's son because he is virtually ageless.

Even when he draws his retirement pension this individual still has a boy's face. But this youthful exterior does nothing to alter the funny old character who has developed over the years, inside. Kindness must be acknowledged, however, for this is basic to his naive nature.

Psychological Significance
This Jack does not take himself seriously and should, therefore, not expect others to do so either. He is amiable, poetic and a day-dreamer, yet becomes bored very quickly. Practical interests should be developed or depression will creep in all too soon.

Psychic Significance
Intuitive and meditative, he has the makings of a good initiate. However, this enthusiasm quickly fades when it is discovered he has to start at the bottom in order to reach the top. Be warned: psychic dabbling could develop if persistence is lacking.

Influential Significance
Without a doubt this influence brings a dash of renewed vigour, especially to a flagging sex life. Such physical rejuvenation surprises everyone and a much more relaxed atmosphere replaces tension, so life will be happier and more fulfilling than of late. Friends rally round and social gatherings provide opportunities for meeting new faces and visiting exciting places.

Reversed Significance
As the unhappy lover of the pack, he makes himself more miserable than is necessary by wallowing in self-pity. This – and pride – prevent him from snapping out of it and, eventually, he takes on the role of the dejected lover, permanently.

TEN OF HEARTS

Numerical Significance
The tenth card in this suit shows that another round of the emotional

side of life has been completed. The culmination of this cycle manifests as inner peace and confidence. A new phase begins soon, built upon the foundations of the past, and plans for the future concerning family, love-affairs and all happy events should be made without delay. Changes are inevitable, but these will be welcomed.

Practical Significance

A very special and pleasant surprise brings happiness and joy. Rewards from past efforts bring unexpected gifts and a happy event. This could be news of a baby, an invitation to a wedding, a family gathering, a party or a reunion with a long-lost friend or lover.

There is a feeling of anticipation in the air, This acts as a protection against negative acts by producing a buffer effect. Progress for the family as a whole is to be expected and inner satisfaction brings long hopes for happiness to the individual. Romantic encounters are on the cards, so lovers can look forward to an especially exciting time when they will be able to devote more time to each other than they thought possible.

Although business and pleasure do not usually mix this is one of the few occasions when one will help the other. Social contacts and entertaining lead to expansion of material benefits, so do not hesitate to invite the boss to dinner. If you are the boss, then give employees a treat and you will be repaid by loyalty in return. This is a time when compassion, friendship and generosity can well be afforded.

Psychological Significance

The prospect of destiny suddenly becomes very important. Inner motives can be examined by deep thinking, yet there is no time for this now because action is needed, not more inaction.

Psychic Significance
A successful cycle, concerned mainly with negative receptivity, mediumship and clairvoyance, has been completed. A change in psychic direction will follow, and this will introduce the more positive side of occultism onto the scene.

Influential Significance
This is a strong protective influence which guards against emotional agony and trauma. Personality clashes will bring no lasting damage and quarrels and misunderstandings will soon be patched up. There is an element of surprise in the air and the introduction of unexpected events will result in much happiness, making life lighter and more relaxing.

Reversed Significance
Romantic opportunities are missed, with a result that self-recrimination follows. Negative emotions create tension which builds up to bursting point. This will clear the air, but also warns that the same unrewarding cycle will begin all over again unless the situation is recognized for what it is and changes made.

NINE OF HEARTS

Numerical Significance
The ninth card in this suit is considered to be the most fortunate in the pack and is known as the 'wish' or 'heart's desire' card. Therefore, all who are concerned with serious love-affairs and matters close to the heart can expect complete fulfilment. As the square of three, this number has stability as its main characteristic. Courage to make romantic approaches and confidence to see things through to the end will suddenly develop as a result of this.

Practical Significance

A high romantic note is reached where the world seems a beautiful place. Since everyone loves a lover, everything in the proverbial garden is lovely too. Those who harbour a secret wish can expect this to come true . . . with just a little effort. Positive steps must be taken to ensure that the desired result is achieved because it takes two to make a bargain.

Apart from these good romantic indications, family affairs will prosper too. An abundance of goodwill flows from within and this affects all who come into contact with it. Life seems really rosy and troubles are at a minimum.

An opportunity will soon be offered to fulfil the heart's desire yet this could be missed unless personal effort is added to it. To a great degree, future happiness depends on the outcome of this opportunity, so be prepared to grasp it with both hands.

Psychological Significance

Solitude becomes a most satisfying experience. Experiencing a complete inner life strengthens purpose and causes illumination to shine into the lesser known, dark corners of the mind. Complete peace of mind brings great happiness.

Psychic Significance

Harmonious relationships between psychics produce excellent results for the good of all living creatures. Healing acts are particularly effective at this time and hopes in this direction will be more than realized.

Influential Significance

This influence is truly romantic. Hidden desires will be ignited and an imminent meeting with a lover is on the cards. Life in general is going to become happier and more exciting as a result of this prevailing atmosphere. Now is the time to make a wish, knowing that it stands a good chance of coming true.

Reversed Significance

The over-romantic atmosphere encourages lovers to make fools of themselves, so beware. Over-enthusiastic behaviour will result in your intentions being misunderstood and the object of the heart's desire will be thoroughly put off. Too much sentimentality, on the other hand, could ruin a plan just as easily as could an overtly sexy approach.

EIGHT OF HEARTS

Numerical Significance

The eighth card in this suit is a paradox because it signifies possibilities which result either in perfect harmony or in bitter disappointment. There are no half measures, so expect all or nothing situations to develop. The difficulty arises when final decisions have to be made; yet, if this can be accomplished, immediate peace of mind is achieved. If friendships are not as satisfying as they should be, now is the time to make a break and start again.

Practical Significance

Happiness is offered, at a price. Superficially, everything appears to be going well but, inwardly, a feeling of emotional uncertainty exists. Apply positivity to the situation and ignore negative signs as much as possible because these are less important than they seem. Forget the past, if possible.

If proffered gifts are accepted as tokens of true affections and not as appeasement presents, any temporary disagreements with family, friends or lovers will soon be forgotten. Social events, romantic moments and sentimental journeys will bring joy to the heart, but again, try to ignore all aspects which threaten to undermine present happiness.

Sensitivity is now at an all-time high, so be careful not to jump to the wrong conclusions, especially where affections are concerned. Feelings of guilt are likely and this could lead to inner conflict. Hasty action will be regretted later, so turn a blind eye to certain things.

Psychological Significance

A split mind exists which takes time to put together again. Deep feelings are at loggerheads and the only way to unite these is to turn your attention to outer, practical aspects where a real solution may be found.

Psychic Significance
A choice between two psychic paths has to be made. This must be decided by the individual, who should in no way be influenced by the group. Forces of equal intensity will make this a difficult decision, however.

Influential Significance
The influence from this card throws new light onto old situations associated with the heart. There are two sides to every question and these will be shown up very clearly. Even so, do not expect to reach conclusions easily because patience will be needed in order to maintain harmony.

Reversed Significance
Prejudice will prevent an alternative course of action from being seen, let alone taken. One-sided views, if allowed to persist, will bring eventual destruction of emotional relationships and leave a void which will be very difficult to fill. Obstacles in the path of love and opposition to sentimental journeys will be virtually impossible to avoid.

SEVEN OF HEARTS

Numerical Significance
The seventh card in this suit is complete within itself and signifies great personal potential for happiness in the future. Everything the heart desires is contained within this card and, provided the game of

life is played according to the rules, wishes and hopes will surely be granted. Self-satisfaction is justifiable for this has been earned as a result of philosophical reactions to life's problems.

Practical Significance

This card represents individual desires for personal happiness and reflects the emotional aspect of the self: that which is known only to the individual concerned. Secrets of the heart suddenly become very important because now is the time to do something about them. Stability has developed from past experience, bring a quiet confidence with its own attractiveness and mystique. So, if this is combined with positive drive, all those romantic dreams can come true. However, if indecision is allowed to creep in, they will, unfortunately, fade all too quickly.

An opportunity will occur shortly which will offer the chance to express artistic talents. This could have far-reaching effects and lead to considerable success or even fame. So now is the time to take stock of dreams and hopes and begin working towards achieving them. New avenues should be explored, too, especially those which bring a diversion from everyday problems.

Psychological Significance

An excess of emotional energy must be allowed to express itself freely or there is a danger of it rebounding as nervous tension. This represents the libido, the basic driving force which, according to Freud, needs a regular sexual outlet.

Psychic Significance

A mystical experience will bring enlightenment and understanding. The symbolism of this signifies a key to the store of unconscious wisdom and, depending on the school of occultism followed, will appear in relation to the Holy Grail, The Tree of Life or the Tao.

Influential Significance

This is a strong personal influence, capable of steering emotional and heartfelt circumstances towards desired conclusions. Compassion and understanding has a calming effect on disturbed individuals and on difficult situations. Lovers may confidently expect a good response from those they desire most and should ensure, therefore, Cupid's dart aims for the right heart.

Reversed Significance
Failure to make the most of a romantic situation will be bitterly regretted. Hopes for a special meeting with someone will be frustrated through lack of initiative and courage. A disappointment in love is on the cards, entirely due to personal neglect and not through lack of opportunity.

SIX OF HEARTS

Numerical Significance
The sixth card in this suit brings the heart's desire nearer, but at a price. Two sets of circumstances are at loggerheads, yet, for peace of mind, they must eventually merge somehow because a compromise is inevitable. One may hope for the best of both worlds but, since this card does not symbolize actual fulfilment but only a step on the way, no immediate conclusion should be expected.

Practical Significance
This card symbolizes some form of self-sacrifice, either self-imposed or the result of unfortunate circumstances. Acceptance is the only answer at this stage, although this does not mean that everything has to remain unchanged. One may be willing to pay a high price for something the heart desires above all else, yet it is foolhardy to take this to the extreme of enforced martyrdom.

To be at the beck and call of the family or having to take a back seat in someone's affections amounts, in principle, to the same thing. A one-sided love-affair or an eternal triangle situation is a notorious breeding ground for willing self-sacrifice.

This card warns that the heart should not be allowed to dictate unconditionally because self-destruction moves in all too quickly, replacing happiness with pain. If this is regarded as a necessary experience then much can be learned but, when looking back on things, nothing should ever be regretted.

Psychological Significance
There is no inner peace at present. Independence is desire but fears of standing alone prevent progress towards this. At least this is an aim in the right direction, so it should become the goal for the future.

Psychic Significance
Psychic abilities should be used in the service of others. This is a testing-time, so expect clairvoyance and all the occult arts to be thoroughly scrutinized and challenged by superiors.

Influential Significance
This is a personal influence which could eventually make a rod for your own back. It allows others to take advantage and exploit your loyalty, yet, at the same time, it encourages the pure sacrificial act which is a gift to those who are genuinely in need of help.

Reversed Significance
Masochistic tendencies attract other people's burdens as well as your own, which will all weigh heavily upon your back. Emotional energy drains away and physical hard work is on the cards too. If this situation is allowed to continue, inner rebellion will cause untold trouble and mental turmoil. Self-help is the first line of defence, therefore.

FIVE OF HEARTS

Numerical Significance
The fifth card in this suit symbolizes the need to communicate with

someone and fulfil that friendship. Sexual relationships, especially on the romantic level, need careful handling because emotions could destroy practical stability and ruin everything. Happiness is encouraged although this could be missed through the implementation of a short-sighted policy. So, play for time: think of tomorrow as well as of today.

Practical Significance
'Still waters run deep' is the message of this card. It signifies a strong urge to escape from true feelings, due to divided loyalties or a guilt complex. The heart and soul have been put into an amorous pursuit at the expense of reason, so caution is needed before all bridges are burnt.

This is a severely testing time when heart-searching questions need honest answers. Actions taken now will have far-reaching effects, and, since these arise from the emotions, considerable restraint is needed. Sexual desires must be strictly controlled or they could be misunderstood. Equally, other strong emotions which also need curbing are those likly to erupt as passionately religious beliefs or nationalistic outbursts.

At this time the truth is difficult to recognize and face. Sometimes it lies beneath excuses which lead to negativity and inaction; at others it manifests in positivity and over-reaction, bordering on extreme fanaticism.

Psychological Significance
Guilt emerges as self-pity one moment and as aggression against others the next. Frustration due to lack of emotional outlets causes a build-up of mental energy which should be released physically, in the form of sex or sport, or expressed mentally through philosophical concepts.

Psychic Significance
A lack of confidence in one's psychic ability brings development to a halt. Communication between the conscious and unconscious mind has been neglected, but the way will open up again once this fact has been recognized.

Influential Significance
This influence encourages one to escape from real issues. It is the 'bury-the-head-in-the-sand' card but, unfortunately, such behaviour will not send troubles packing. A brave heart is needed above all else.

Strength seems to gather from nowhere once the world has been faced because others will then make moves which will help to improve the situation tremendously. The first move must, however, come from within the individual.

Reversed Significance
Turning a blind eye to personal affairs presents others with the opportunity to take unfair advantage. Laziness plus cowardice heaps more troubles on the old ones, so there is an urgent need for a change in direction. Heaven-sent opportunities still arise but are consistently ignored.

FOUR OF HEARTS

Numerical Significance
The fourth card in this suit tugs at the emotional heart-strings. There is a fear of toppling too far one way so that life appears to be rather like walking a tightrope just now. Beware of jumping out of the frying pan into the fire, yet, at the same time, do not simply sit there: something must be done but the question is, what and when?

Practical Significance
Emotional independence is represented by this card. This has developed not so much from happiness but more through painful experiences which tore at the strings themselves. Having reached this singular stage, fear of showing one's true feelings exist and emotions now act as a barrier which keep romantic encounters at bay as a result. Members of the opposite sex are viewed with distinct mistrust and lack of confidence in them and oneself has formed a negative alliance.

In family circles disharmony rules. Arguments and disagreements may well give cause for concern yet, if this situation is faced fairly and squarely, much of the heat can be removed and things will then be able to simmer down generally.

Swinging from the heights to the depths emotionally makes for unstable situations and relationships, so this is not the time to make bold decisions which could very well be regretted later. It would be better to do nothing than to spoil the future but, if action is unavoidable, try to take steps which are not guided solely by the heart's wishes. Remember, the head should have its say too.

Psychological Significance
Swinging emotions produce manic-depressive moods. If external circumstances are to blame, concentrate on keeping a middle of the road course. If it is inner feelings which colour and trigger matters off, learn to recognize the two extremes of temperament and blend them mentally.

Psychic Significance
The importance of the four-fold nature of matter is indicated with this card. This suit represents water which, in turn, symbolizes compassion, understanding and feeling for others. The further development of these qualities is needed before a four-square psychic footing can be achieved, however.

Influential Significance
This has an unsettling influence on the emotions. Its origin is found in past bitter experience which is best forgotten if future happiness is ever to be won. Sometimes is provides protection against complicated love affairs; at others it opens the door onto one-sided relationships which drag on to become forlorn romantic hopes. Sit tight and wait for the winds of change to blow.

Reversed Significance
Unfair deals in love bring inner misery. Nothing will ever happen to change things, therefore it is advisable to try to forget the past, accept the present and plan for a better future. Familiarity breeds contempt, so do not make this mistake on top of all others.

THREE OF HEARTS

Numerical Significance
The third card in this suit shows emotional stability with considerable

control over personal feelings. A quiet confidence attracts others of like natures and a new-found emotional stability increases attractiveness, so lovers should find life particularly fulfilling. Friends and family appear more amenable than usual and everything goes smoothly and swimmingly.

Those who are madly in love can expect a reward for their devotions and one way in which this expresses itself is in an increase from two to three. A new baby could be the one to make up this number . . . so be prepared.

Fertility of imagination is also ready to produce its brain child which, like its physical symbolic counterpart, is full of potential and hope for the future. It is as if a long period of training is over and, having completed the course of sowing, the reaping is about to begin. What follows is the harvest: a prize of which to be truly proud. Abundance of emotional happiness should be stored and treasured for a rainy day.

Psychological Significance
Emotional stability has been won through personal effort. This is a superior mental state which bestows strength of purpose to aims and ambitions of a practical nature. Expect progress with underlying plans.

Psychic Significance
The still, inner voice of intuition should always be heeded and respected. Original psychic techniques and unique remedies for healing arise from this source.

Influential Significance
This influence restores any lack of self-confidence. If there is a yearning for a particular partner then this new-found inner stability

will attract him or her in the right direction. A surplus of mental energy creates a much more stable atmosphere, so life should grow happier and easier all round.

Reversed Significance
Emotional effort is wasted in the wrong direction. Relationships prove most unsatisfactory owing to poor judgment of character. Lovers and friends seem unreliable, but the truth is that the fault lies much nearer home. Do not take sides in three-cornered arguments where no one can win.

TWO OF HEARTS

Numerical Significance
The second card in this suit holds the key to harmonious relationships where two hearts beat as one. Whether two can live as cheaply as one is another matter however, so the diamonds and clubs must be consulted in this respect. Individually, a good relationship has developed between the inner and outer selves, resulting in a much more expansive outlook on life.

Practical Significance
Marriage and all romantic partnership are represented by this card. Chance meetings and renewed acquaintances will blossom into deep and happy friendships, some ending in marriage, others not. All sexual relationships – from the first kiss to the finality of making love – are also symbolized by the two hearts on this one card. Plenty of give and take, partners in themselves, are needed to maintain this delicate balance, but this can be done quite successfully when there is a joint aim.

Apart from lovers, relationships between friends, neighbours, workmates and family flourish, so there should be plenty of fairness and equality all round. This is a good time to iron out any difference and long-standing disagreements. Such troubles may well come to a head, so be ready to deal with them with a compassionate heart.

The merging of ideas will more than double the rewards and you should not let pride keep progress from the door any longer than needs be. This is the time to unite in theory, if not in practice.

Psychological Significance
A natural sense of justice and fair play paves the way for a greater understanding of action and reaction, sowing and reaping, Yin and Yang. These are the basic principles of psychology as well as those of the universe as a whole and produce inner peace as well as an out atmosphere of harmony.

Psychic Significance
Telepathy between well balanced psychic partners leads to further occult initiations. Working in pairs will increase awareness safely and surely as long as a unified aim exists.

Influential Significance
This is a dual influence affecting hearts and emotions. The opportunity for shared romance and joint happiness is offered, probably arising from social activities or holidays. A generally peaceful atmosphere reigns, allowing time to rest and catch up on the more neglected aspects of family life. Shared experiences bring joy and laughter.

Reversed Significance
Disharmony between lovers, friends and family is on the cards. Emotional relationships are very unstable and disagreement all round makes life intolerable. Revealing personal feelings to others will lead to further misunderstandings and only make matters worse.

SPADES

ACE OF SPADES

Numerical Significance
This is the first and last card in this suit and combines numbers one and thirteen into a source of trouble. This is seen as a necessary evil because it brings into the open that which festers beneath the surface. The force behind this has the power to leave no stone unturned and in so doing reveals some pretty unpleasant surprises.

Practical Significance
An enormous hurdle or challenge in life lies in this card. It brings to a close one phase and starts off the next so this is why it is often seen as the death card. Life is staged throughout in phases and many of these end on climactic notes; the symbolic death of a love-affair is one such example. Death, therefore, is by no means the only finality we have to face, as this card signifies.

Underlying problems relating to health, business, money matters, love-affairs, ambitions, careers and hopes for the future will be affected and are bound to come to a head soon. Action will be forced upon those who ignore the warning signs so be prepared. A sense of justice rules too, which often appears ruthless for the natural

82

law of action and reaction does not take feelings into account. On a practical level, law suits are possible concerning tussles over rights and possessions, but a philosophical approach, where everything is fair in love and war, helps soften such blows. So face up to the challenge and, where necessary, accept these events as inevitable stumbling blocks along life's highway.

Psychological Significance
A mental hang-up prevents real enjoyment, satisfaction and happiness from life. This is the iceberg of the mind where only the tip shows and the rest lies dangerously submerged beneath the surface of the unconscious. The first step towards thawing out this condition is to accept its existence and know its extent.

Psychic Significance
Beware of unseen dangers. Occult attacks through foolhardiness could bring fear and trepidation to even the most experienced psychic workers. Keep up protection and challenge every entity and force thoroughly. The effects from this cause disharmony within the group and loss of confidence in the individual.

Influential Significance
This influence adds fuel to the fire that needs just a spark to set off an inferno. Once this happens it must be fought with might and main. It has the power to disrupt situations and turn placid people into aggressive lunatics who collectively start riots and even wars.

Reversed Significance
If things could get worse then they will. Forsaken by friends and life generally, injustices appear on all fronts producing a trap from which escape seems impossible. Enormous personal effort is needed to alter the present downward trend where problems are forming into immovable obstacles.

KING OF SPADES

The King's Significance
This King is the archetypal judge attracted to authoritarian positions in life. He is often found in local government, politics and the professions, especially law. Dogmatic and severely critical, he is quick to see faults in others but fails to notice his own. With a ruthless logic devoid of all compassion his intellect rules stubbornly over his

instinct and intuition. It is better to have him as a friend than a foe.

Practical Significance

Energy surrounds this dominant and positive character. He uses this ruthlessly and unstintingly to further his own ends and once he is on the ladder of success he means to stay there until he reaches the top. He is most professional in everything he does and nothing short of perfection, often at the expense of others, will do. This leaves no room for the slightest criticism from others but, to be fair, he does his job very well indeed.

When at work he crosses swords with everyone who stands in his way. Since popularity does not go with either his job or his character he remains a loner. There are two types of women who are attracted to him; the masochist who enjoys being the underdog and the more than equal female who means to be top dog. She controls him from the start, much to everyone's delight and surprise.

Beneath the armour of over-confidence and self-opinionated superiority there actually lies a streak of insecurity. To cover this up he over-reacts and, in so doing, reveals his weakness.

Psychological Significance

There is a danger of a dynamic personality being ruined in later years through greed. In pursuit of power, patriarchal tendencies could become tyrannical but if these are tempered with wisdom, true leadership qualities emerge. Cruel traits exist which must be curbed.

Psychic Significance

Striving to invoke the four elements, this potential wizard or warlock seeks power and not wisdom. By contacting forces which he later finds to be beyond his control, he eventually falls under their spell although would never admit this.

84

Influential Significance
This influence produces single-mindedness and a ruthless approach to life. It gives power to enforce decisions and law and order which, in certain circumstances, is essential. There is always the danger of overstepping the mark and becoming too dicatatorial, so the utmost discretion is needed.

Reversed Significance
A lonely destiny lies ahead for this cold, calculating character. Pursuits of power have led him along a path strewn with obstacles and trouble which eventually build up into insurmountable barriers. Chaos and disorder rule completely.

QUEEN OF SPADES

The Queen's Significance
This Queen is ambitious and ruthless in pursuit of power. She rules the roost wherever and whenever she can and makes others well aware of their subordinate pecking order. A stickler for discipline she rarely takes other people's feelings into account when she lays down the law. Thinking exclusively with her head enables her to achieve feats more sensitive women would never desire, let alone strive for.

Practical Significance
There is no need for an enemy with a friend like this woman. Friends to her are there to do her bidding and nothing else, but she loses most of these after their first encounter with her selfish temperament. Committee work attracts her and it is not long before she takes command, including the chair. Since she is far from stupid she plays her cards right from the start, so it is not really surprising that she is

applauded for her organizing abilities and devotion to the cause.

This Queen is sure to be found in every office and place of work. Age does not matter, for both young and old alike play the same overbearing role, with the result that they are known as witches and worse. Regarded as a diffficult, bossy and thoroughly dangerous woman she sees herself as a dutiful, honest and forthright person who is greatly wronged by everyone, including her family.

Psychological Significance

Hard-hearted and headstrong this character lacks every trace of feminine warmth. Inhibited emotions cause frustration which adds to the outer veneer of ruthlessness. A close relationship with the opposite sex is desperately needed, but there are few men who feel inclined to take her on. When they do the partnership does not last long.

Psychic Significance

In the past this Queen would have been recognized as a witch whose practices were suspect to say the least. Considerable occult knowledge gives her power over those who become her initiates and, once in her clutches, it is virtually impossible to escape.

Influential Significance

This is a ruthless influence lacking all compassion and wisdom. It is reminiscent of the iron hand in the velvet glove which delivers blows swiftly and passes on silently leaving behind confusion and disruption. Good may result from this havoc eventually, but this will depend on other factors as well. Beware of the person who helps others into trouble.

Reversed Significance

Selfishness develops into a rigid characteristic that blots out every trace of feeling for others. As a female recluse, everyone keeps well away for fear of being attacked verbally, if not physically. Loneliness is inevitable, but this woman is her own worst enemy.

JACK OF SPADES

The Jack's Significance

This card rarely represents a boy but if it does it depicts a delinquent. As a man it symbolizes an emotionally immature, inadequate and totally impractical person. He is misinformed and is misinforming

so his word and advice should never be relied upon. Even so, he is full of self-importance, self-confidence and big ideas. As he grows older he lives more and more in a world of his own.

Practical Significance
Although this man lacks authority, he takes it upon himself to boss others. This does not make for popularity but he has only himself to blame. Insincerity in the past has given him a bad reputation, so when it comes to promotion at work he is passed over. Friends are few and far between but, since 'birds of a feather flock together', those he has are unreliable and devious. They are the proverbial dogs who have been given a bad name so it is difficult to shake off this bad image. This Jack is usually the leader of the gang.

As a husband he is hard going for any woman who is foolish enough to have him. A Queen of spades is the only one who has any degree of control over him, but this is never a happy arrangement. Should a romantic Queen of hearts misguidedly take him on, she will rue the day and every succeeding day she stays with him. His mother and older women are the only ones who have any time for him. Maybe this is because his mentality remains that of a spoilt child all his life.

Psychological Significance
Gross emotional immaturity is the cause of this mixed-up character. Inner turmoil manifests outwardly as aggression and wanton behaviour. Leadership qualities are only temporary and disappear altogether with increasing years.

Psychic Significance
Entering the psychic scene like a flash of lightning, all attention focusses on this startling newcomer. But thunder will surely follow

and these rumblings should arouse suspicions, so beware of him. He will certainly have a few tricks up his sleeve, but only the naive and gullible will be taken in.

Influential Significance
This disturbing influence brings out the worst in individuals and agnifies the negative aspects in every situation. Everything will be revealed through this, so expect secrets to be thrown to the wind and confidences to be broken. Courage is needed to face up to all this, but to compensate there is a feeling of distinct relief.

Reversed Significance
A thoroughly despicable character like this should not expect much from anyone. Untrustworthy and unreliable he is shunned and lonely. At work he is avoided and in the home he receives little love since he gives little in return. When confronted with his own mistakes and faults he flies into a childish rage.

TEN OF SPADES

Numerical Significance
The tenth card in this suit completes a round in life which has been difficult to say the least. From this point things can only get better. Looking back on events shows how things went in circles with nothing accomplished in the end. Even a downward spiral may be discovered, from which it will take time to recover, but as an obstacle course this phase has ended.

Practical Significance
Personal frustration is to be expected as a result of past and present circumstances, so tears and jealousy are excusable although they do nothing to solve things. Enthusiasm and hopes are likely to be

dashed to the ground so do not expect too much yet. Difficulties with practical plans, emotional hopes and money matters bring delays and minor upsets. Communication proves to be a major problem which causes misunderstandings all round.

Loss of jobs and failure to find new ones take their toll on emotions and domestic scenes suffer from intolerance and frayed nerves as a result. Relationships naturally become tense so watch out for trouble spots which trigger off fiery reactions. This is generally a negative card; therefore every possible precaution should be taken, on every level, to keep things on an even keel. This will be a lone task and it will be difficult to recognize true friends but, if it is of any comfort, many are in the same boat with you. An end to the present trouble is in sight, so keep going.

Psychological Significance
Depths of depression are reached through external circumstances. This is understandable but it must not develop into a regular response pattern where every obstacle, however small, triggers off this extremely negative reaction.

Psychic Significance
Occult work in a group faces a severe challenge. The weakest link in the chain places everyone in danger, so whoever this person is must be discovered, psychically cleared and re-aligned. Strengthen protection against external, interfering forces which seek to break up a circle trying to work harmoniously.

Influential Significance
Enthusiasm will be drastically dampened down by this negative influence. Any lack of drive must be fought and overcome if survival on practical, emotional and financial fronts is to be maintained. Stick to original plans until something better turns up, which it will shortly. Beware of misunderstanding which could trigger off a long chain of events which blight the future.

Reversed Significance
Just when things look to be at their worst they deteriorate even more. A rough ride, going over the same old ground frustrates to breaking point. It is difficult to see where all this will lead as the wheel of fate continues to turn much as it did before.

NINE OF SPADES

Numerical Significance
The ninth card in this suit is consistant in that it keeps up its promise of further negativity. An all-time low is reached which affects any one of the three other suits representing practical, emotional and financial matters. Even so, everything happening now helps to clear the air but this will be realized only after the event and when the edge has worn off a painful memory. Numerically, it is still a fortunate number if only because it prevents an even worse fate.

Practical Significance
Worries over health and, to a lesser extent, wealth drain energy, allowing depression to take over. A stage is reached where action must be taken so whatever happens, expect something of a change. Illnesses will be brought to light and revealed for what they are; these range from minor complaints to conditions needing urgent medical attention. Suspense comes to an end with this comparative peace of mind, as long-feared enemies are recognized for what they are.

Scandals and idle gossip bring unhappiness to many innocent people. Although this could result a long time after the event which started off the negative trail, it still causes suffering. It is important to try to rise above these difficult circumstances, as impossible as it seems and above all, conserve personal energy. This is the key to solving all trouble, physical and mental, so rest and relax whenever possible. Beware of wasting valuable energy on trivialities that do not really matter and ignore pettiness in others for this is a trap which distracts from the main issue.

Psychological Significance
Lack of energy lowers resistance to everything. Apart from feeling

under the weather physically, the emotional threshold to stress is so weakened that a break-down is on the cards. It is far better to do nothing rather than do the wrong thing, because this simply piles on the agony.

Psychic Significance
Occult battles with negative forces test defences. Rituals involving astral projection should not be attempted at this stage for fear of a serious attack. Watch out for danger signals inside as well as outside the group or circle, which seek to cause a rift.

Influential Significance
As a negative influence of a parasitic nature this will deplete even the strongest characters. Beware of wasting energy on self-pity and self-recrimination as a result of this; instead, reverse the process into positive thinking and planning. Tiredness and lack of drive unite into a destructive partnership and, if allowed to continue, they demolish every hope for the future.

Reversed Significance
Serious troubles associated with poor health and lack of wealth bring increasing bouts of depression. Help is no longer offered because it has been rejected in the past. Underhand schemes to make money fail and, even worse, past devious plans designed to extract profits by undesirable means will be exposed. Further misery results.

EIGHT OF SPADES

Numerical Significance
The eighth card in this suit is negative and most unfortunate, causing

disputes which are extremely difficult to understand, let alone resolve. This is because only half the picture can be seen at any one time and somewhere between the two lies a no man's land where there is nothing to win and nothing to lose either. This is a thoroughly frustrating situation which cannot be ignored.

Practical Significance

Obstacles and indecisions rule over every aspect of life. Business schemes, travel arrangements, including holidays and ambitions for the future suffer particularly so expect delays before matters are sorted out satisfactorily. In arguments, both points of view are evenly matched, making it virtually impossible to make progress but, sooner or later, the scales will tip one way and end the present deadlock. Time must not be wasted during this temporary lull, so use this to prepare for the final fray and the action which is bound to follow. No good will come from forcing the issue at this stage so sit tight.

On the domestic front there will be clashes within the family probably between younger and older members. Love-affairs will face a testing time too and only the really well adjusted relationships will survive. A strong warning is also given with this card concerning trust. Do not reveal personal secrets nor give away confidential information relating to other people to anyone.

There is a possibility of enforced isolation such as a stay in hospital or, in extreme cases, it could be a prison sentence. Whichever it is, this should be taken as an opportunity to recover from personal difficulties. It will also act as a future safeguard and protection.

Psychological Significance

Definite strength of will exists, but without a specific aim this is like a journey without a destination. Make sure that an end object is in view and that mental energy is properly controlled and directed towards this. Intellectual powers will be wasted too, unless a strict discipline and routine is laid down and kept to.

Psychic Significance

Beware of working in the dark both literally and metaphorically. Lone workers are in particular danger of an occult attack since they lack protection from a psychic partner or from a group. These attacks will take unexpected and unusual forms and will by no means be confined to psychic levels only.

Influential Significance
This influence frustrates the individual by placing obstacles in the way and brings wheels within wheels grinding to a halt. Attempts to communicate with others fail, so take advantage of this uneasy quiet to make watertight plans and better policies in readiness. Strained emotional relationships run the risk of reaching breaking point, especially if enemies have a chance to have their say.

Reversed Significance
No good will come from a scheme, in spite of all the effort and hard work put into it. This leads to despondency, depression and dejection which does not lift easily. Lack of self-confidence does little to help an already bad situation.

SEVEN OF SPADES

Numerical Significance
The seventh card in this suit has strong personal associations of a distinctly negative nature. Secret fears and worries cast despondent shadows over the brightest scenes and bad characteristics are allowed to express themselves. These override compassion from the heart and logic from the head. Individual selfishness rules and will continue to do so until a realistic and honest approach to life is adopted.

Practical Significance
Although personal worries exist, they are no excuse for bad manners and hasty tempers. By allowing fears of what might happen to control and colour every aspect of life, a dark cloud hangs over the present. Eventually this will bring a depletion of energy, and invite

more trouble in the form of physical illness and depression.

There is a risk that attitudes to life become increasingly selfish and, although rarely recognized as this, other people see it all too clearly. Negative situations are attracted to negative people, so much of the present trouble could have been avoided. Practical and emotional problems may well exist but these can become complicated through wrong thinking and consequent wrong handling. Disputes with friends and workmates are unavoidable and these strike deep at the roots of individual standpoint. Obstacles and misfortunes, however, are necessary experiences meant to teach lessons in living, but the present chain of negative events is being fostered by a poor philosophy and understanding of what life is all about.

Psychological Significance
Difficulty in altering fixed patterns of thought form a barrier around the mind which blinkers the sight. Expansion and expression of the personality is inhibited and an altogether bigoted character develops. If freed from this self-imposed bond, a new positive life-style develops and one way to begin to do this is to seek out a good basic philosophy.

Psychic Significance
Insufficient belief in powers beyond this world must be reconciled with the continued pursuit of psychic phenomena. It is extremely dangerous to venture further along the occult path without complete acceptance of these, plus recognition of symbols and archetypes. Rebound reactions are to be expected until a definite conclusion is reached.

Influential Significance
Personal problems reach a crisis point as a result of this influence. Worries concerning health, the family or matters at work cast gloom over everything else. Fears will be exaggerated and although most of these will never happen, they still have the power to produce a negative atmosphere and interfere with peace of mind. Control has never been more necessary than now, because things could deteriorate even more if left to their own devices.

Reversed Significance
Spite and malice are fostered like vipers in the bosom. Seeing life as an errand of vengeance can only reap more disasterous reactions, so

until it is realized that one negative action produces another negative reaction, things will continue on the downward path until rock-bottom is reached.

SIX OF SPADES

Numerical Significance
The sixth card in this suit represent hard work which shows little reward for all the effort. Attempts to preserve that which has already been achieved will meet with opposition, but the fight must continue. There are always two aspects to be considered and these have to be manoeuvred into a position which produces some degree of equilibrium.

Practical Significance
Disappointments are inevitable, but this does not mean all is lost. Although a 'wet blanket' atmosphere dampens down enthusiasm, in no way does it extinguish the spark of ingenuity so there is still hope. Set-backs such as this, when viewed in retrospect, will be seen to have been for the best.

Minor health problems will prevent complete fulfilment of plans, but again, all will be for the best so do not waste time and energy worrying about what might have been. Depression is likely but this should not be allowed to overshadow the hatching of plans for the future. From a practical point of view, just when contracts concerning property are about to be signed, along come doubts and everything stops short. Diplomacy and time will work wonders in this situation whereas attempts to force the issue will only make things worse. Have faith and wait for a change in circumstances which will be for the better.

Psychological Significance
Difficulties in reconciling the inner realm of dreams with the outer world of harsh realities causes mental conflict. One without the other is incomplete and therefore unfulfilling, so the answer lies in a blend of the two. These two aspects represent the conscious and unconscious minds, between which there should exist strong links.

Psychic Significance
Forces beyond control impose self-sacrifice that greatly disturb psychic workers. Those who operate alone are in particular danger. Difficulties with astral projection will be the first warning sign, followed by garbled messages from outer space.

Influential Significance
This influence brings disappointment, tears and set-backs. Even when things seem to be going really well, a negative feeling manages to creep in and spoil everything. Undercover actions are suspected although there is no proof that they exist. Matters will improve shortly but meanwhile, be prepared for delays, unexpected obstacles and being let down by others.

Reversed Significance
News which should have arrived some time ago arrives too late to prevent a catastrophe. Obstacles now seem like permanent fixtures and trying to escape them is impossible, certainly at the moment. A long chain of disasters, fortunately none of which are devastating, look like continuing for some time.

FIVE OF SPADES

Numerical Significance

The fifth card in this suit has the power to demolish every hope that once stood a good chance of succeeding. Misunderstandings and misinterpretations have laid a false trail leading to the downward path. Aims and ambitions for the future must not be lost, in spite of the present obstacles because this is a testing-time. Those who emerge will greatly increase their strength and understanding of life. Personal involvement with certain unpleasant situations cannot be avoided and it will mean carrying other people's burdens.

Practical Significance

This card warns against discouragement. Although trouble seems to heap upon trouble, there is still a bright spot on the horizon. Success is still within the grasp, so long as it is sought with courage and determination. Whatever the odds, try hard to see it through to the end and do not give up now.

Plans for a career, business projects, holidays and moving house are all at risk due to temporary set-backs, but last minute reprieves suddenly put everything right again.

Money matters take a knocking but again final calculations will show them to be far better than was feared. On the emotional level, relationships will suffer from misunderstandings which complicate things so much that there is a risk of a complete break. By accepting the inevitable and flowing with the stream there will be an improvement of circumstances, but do not expect to solve difficulties easily for this is impossible. Original plans and hopes should not be allowed to become submerged beneath the present trouble. Confidence and strength is needed to carry on, so concentrate on the future and not on past regrets. Accept that everything is going to take that much longer than was first thought and reorganize the calendar to fit in with the new schedule. Once this is done there will be a feeling of relief at having tried to do something about the situation.

Psychological Significance

Beware of speaking your mind in the so-called name of honesty. Brutal truths should be delivered with discretion and more often than not they should be replaced with white lies anyway. It is not a sign of a strong character to be able to tell others their fortunes in this way.

Psychic Significance

Entities from the lower astral plane masquerade as innocent spirits.

These test the power of challenge and call for accurate recognition of signs, symbols, archetypes and all unseen forces. Use the pentacle, the five-pointed star, for protection.

Influential Significance
This influence has the power to complicate and disrupt even the simplest of plans. On the positive side it will single out unseen obstacles which are better brought to light now than later so in this sense it is not bad. Eventual success is on the cards, but only after difficulties have been ironed out. Doubt and lack of faith in ones own ability is also introduced with this influence so see it as a real personal challenge.

Reversed Significance
Beware of the stab in the back which could have far-reaching disastrous effects. This may result from the past, so try to put an end to a negative chain of events before it reaps more havoc. Legal battles will prove costly and in the end nothing will have been proved. Try to avoid such action.

FOUR OF SPADES

Numerical Significance
The fourth card in this suit combines an unstable number with the negativity of the suit as a whole. The effect from this is to halt previous progress in different ways and create trouble all round. Battles are foreseen and these range from court cases down to battles of wits.

Practical Significance
Legal battles, arguments and disputes are to be expected. Watertight

cases suddenly spring a leak and everything looks like collapsing. The weakest link in the chain should be found and examined carefully for signs of trouble and, small though these may be, they have the power to wreck everything. Practical, emotional and financial plans will all be affected. Love-affairs will develop into frustrating experiences especially if clandestine meetings are involved. As a warning, divorce or separation is on the cards. Unfortunately, there is little one can do about the present situation except wait and see.

A rest from worry and strife should be considered, which is not the same as trying to escape personal responsibilities. Health problems could be an added burden so this must be preserved above all else. Loss of sleep from a worry could start a vicious circle, ending in either physical or mental illness, so make sure a good night's rest is a regular occurrence. Relax during the day-time whenever possible.

Psychological Significance
Primitive instincts should be recognized as such and therefore controlled. These go with mundane pursuits and whilst they continue to rule, intellect and wisdom, let alone compassion, do not have a look-in. Brute force and ignorance lead to self-imposed imprisonment.

Psychic Significance
Be prepared for a battle with occult forces. Difficulties in knowing the enemy, who will be heavily disguised, confuse and disrupt the harmony within the group. Long-term after-effects will further disturb and bring trouble but at least it will sort the sheep from the goats.

Influential Signficance
This influence introduces a heartless atmosphere. Disputes arising from business and matrimonial affairs could end in court and in lengthy legal battles. On a less formidable level, troubles will be brought into the open where they can be dealt with fairly and squarely. Although unpleasant at the time, the air will be cleared as a result.

Reversed Significance
Lack of courage does nothing to help the present wave of trouble. Ignoring the true facts only postpones the final outcome and this

gets worse the longer it is left. Delaying tactics should not be tried and although this may seem one way out it is, in fact, only putting off the evil moment.

THREE OF SPADES

Numerical Significance
The third card in this suit represents a three-sided problem which undermines stability and equality. Emotional relationships and business partnerships are particularly susceptible as a third person or principle tries to interfere with the present harmony. Destructive forces seek to destroy long-established arrangements and will often try to do this in the name of progress.

Practical Significance
This card symbolizes the eternal triangle, a situation that can never be a happy arrangement. When relating to marriage and business partnerships no stability or progress will ever be made whilst this unsatisfasctory structure exists. A blind eye may be turned to an ever increasing threat but this cannot be swept under the carpet forever. Evntually, the truth will out.

As a warning, every precaution should be taken when considering a third partner for he or she may sooner or later throw a spanner in the works. On emotional levels a third person enters the scene who has the power to disrupt an old-established relationship. This is usually presumed to be a secret lover but the culprit might be a child or relative who proves the theory that two are company but three is a crowd. Even an obsession which one of the partners has for a hobby or sport could be the third interloper but whoever or whatever it is, it will take three times as much effort to keep the status quo.

Psychological Significance
Creative thoughts are self-inhibited so the result is third-rate work and lack of originality. A complete change in attitude, not only to work but to life as a whole is needed, but this must be voluntary and not something imposed by a third party.

Psychic Significance
Beware of matriarchal tyranny ruling through emotional blackmail, mental enslavement and jealousy. This will be cleverly done so do not expect the obvious. Feminine vibrations of a destructive nature must be anticipated and, as destructive as these are, they will not be easily recognized.

Influential Significance
This influence introduces a third aspect which thoroughly upsets plans and relationships. Arguments develop and there is the likelihood of great enmity stemming from a once harmonious situation. The breaking of agreements is likely and applies to emotional commitments as well as to business pledges. As an early warning sign look for an atmosphere of aggression.

Reversed Significance
The breaking of an agreement can lead to personal strife and collectively to group or even national hostility. Action of a most despicable nature is taken and this is not done in the name of humanity. Disorder rules in place of harmony, so the future looks bleak and without a lot of hope for some time to come.

TWO OF SPADES

Numerical Significance

The second card in this suit brings duality and opposition. Complications arise and the disharmony produced by this has the power to sever long-standing relationships and agreements. Indecision delays everything with stalemate situations on emotional, practical and financial fronts. Neither side of the fence offers a balanced solution so wait for further developments before taking the next step.

Practical Significance

This card warns of a dividing of the ways but there is little to choose from either path. Split into two, neither half is complete within itself so difficulties will undoubtedly develop. These will grow unless the situation is faced, understood and accepted. Then, and only then should further moves be considered. A change in direction will bring the present stalemate to an end but determination and patience are needed to do this. Expect the depths of depression on the one hand, but hope on the other because from this point the only way out is up.

Emotional relationships will be charged with disharmony through clashes of temperament and business partnerships will suffer from opposing views. Separate ways are on the cards but there is no reason why these paths should not unite in the future when both parties are on the same track again.

Since this card represents an all-time low everything associated with it can only be described as negative too. Seen symbolically as the last week of winter, spring cannot be far behind.

Psychological Significance

Obsessions reach a peak or trough, as the case may be. The truth is distorted out of all proportion as complete fantasy takes over. There is a danger of entering a dream world from which there is no escape and no return.

Psychic Significance

The dangers of evoking names of power are realized too late. Dual forces clash causing psychic fireworks and a chain reaction is started which encircles and enslaves those who first sought to raise them.

Influential Significance

This influence negates and opposes all hopes and plans for the future. Indecisions and uncertainty shatter personal confidence, so balanced outlooks suddenly suffer a split down the middle causing confusion and depression. In all relationships, both sides will find that this influence highlights their partners defects which leads to more trouble. Since plans become impossible to fulfil and finances are greatly reduced, hibernate mentally and wait for the first breath of spring.

Reversed Significance

This card represents the depths of depression and despair. Deliberate and downright bad intentions have produced negativity, so gloom and darkness overshadows everything. As the dark night of the soul, all hope seems to have gone but a final chance to redress the balance will be offered soon.

THE JOKER

The Joker's Significance

This card is not numbered but traditionally it is represented as zero, a sign embracing all and nothing, sense and nonsense, happiness and sadness and wisdom and folly. Looking at this lively figure it is difficult to decide exactly what his message is until, that is, it is realized that he is in disguise. His costume is that of a court jester, a buffoon who was supposed to make a King laugh. A jester, however, was far from a fool and in this lies the Joker's secret.

Practical Significance

This card symbolizes individual potential latent within each of us which may or may not express itself fully during one lifetime. On the surface, this appears as the innocence of a child, the wisdom of Job, the stupidity of an idiot or as pure tomfoolery but whichever it is, it has the power to deceive and take others by surprise.

Progress in practical and financial affairs can confidently be expected as unlimited energy drives on towards a most satisfactory conclusion. Powers to transform are at work so anything is possible as new life is given to flagging projects. Emotionally, an unexpected experience has a profound effect on relationships and, whether happy or disillusioning, it certainly throws a new light onto the whole affair. Intellectually, a flash of brilliance and originality brings success to those striving for academic awards and again, this comes out of the blue.

Untapped energy and individual possibilities express themselves when least expected with a result that lives and situations could be transformed overnight. A carefree attitude replaces an old cautious approach, making life much easier to face, if nothing else.

Psychological Significance

Here is the eccentric who harbours the seeds of a genius but these will grow only if sown in a conventional way. In doing this lies the difficulty. Unable to accept society as it is, he or she attempts to alter it but, since this cannot be done without first becoming part of that establishment, the task seems impossible. The Joker, however, is a clever juggler too and takes everyone, including himself, by surprise!

Psychic Significance

A psychic awakening opens the door on a new dimension and the journey into another world has begun. Seeking enlightenment in this way reveals the path of the mystic and this is one strewn with pitfalls and rewards but, above all, surprises.

Influential Significance

Expect the unexpected with this influence. Surprises will alter situations in a flash, bringing last minute help, changes in fortune, recovery from illnesses and instant friendship, both platonic as well as romantic. Be prepared for sudden illogical events involving people and circumstances that are most unusual and perhaps comical.

Reversed Significance

Living up to the ordinary reputation of the Joker, expect status to be downgraded to the level of a fool, a vagbond and a mindless seeker of pleasure. There is indeed nothing much of a character beneath a superficial top dressing.

PART TWO

FORTUNE-TELLING

with

TAROT CARDS

4
RITUAL AND PROCEDURE

Looking After the Cards
Tarot cards which are meant to be used for divination should not be used for card games. They should be kept either in their box or in a drawstring bag. Many professional readers like to wrap their cards in a silk scarf to insulate the cards from outside influences. I have never done this, I just keep them in their box. The cards should be used only by you, the Reader, except when being shuffled by the Questioner prior to a reading. Other people should not be allowed to mess about with them or they will pick up too many cross-vibrations.

New Cards
It is a good idea to 'work up' a new pack by laying each card on top of the same cards from an old deck. If you have no old deck of your own, then be careful whose deck you use for this. If this idea does not appeal to you, then just keep on shuffling the cards and doing some test readings for yourself and your family until they lose their newness.

Guidelines for Readers
Always be careful not to frighten a Questioner when you are giving a reading. Most people tend to take what is said to them very seriously, even if they are outwardly sceptical or even derisory. It would be unforgivable to frighten or upset someone needlessly. Even a very experienced professional Reader has to take care when giving bad news, but in the case of an absolute beginner, if your Questioner should happen to pick out a set of really black cards, I would actually advise you to tone your interpretation right down, even to the point of risking your credibility. If you maintain your interest in the Tarot, you will soon learn to judge people and develop an instinct for giving bad news tactfully but confidently.

People are funny; the majority of us are quite happy to be gently

108

For a reading using upright and reversed cards
The Questioner cuts the cards into three decks
and then chooses one of them.

The Reader turns the deck which the Questioner has chosen.

The end which was nearest to the Questioner must be placed
nearest to the Reader.

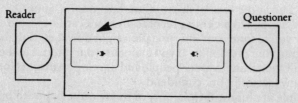

criticized by a Reader, we also enjoy being told that we have had a lot to put up with in the past (who hasn't?). We don't even mind being told that we will have to face a few more problems in the future, but we really hate to hear of specific health problems, troubles affecting out children, or that a loved one is being unfaithful. So as a Reader, even if you are absolutely convinced that the Questioner sitting in front of you has a youngster who will soon be in trouble with the law, a spouse who is putting it about and a really majestic cancer growing right in the middle of his middle – do yourself a favour, tone it all down a little!

Dealing the Cards

When you are ready to try a reading, sit somewhere quiet and comfortable. Use a table which is large enough to spread the cards out on; the dining table is often a popular place for this. Shuffle the cards a little if you wish, then pass them on to the Questioner and let him or her give them a good shuffle. Ask the Questioner to cut the cards into three decks, using the left hand (nearest to the heart). If you wish to give an upright and reversed reading, you can also ask the Questioner to choose one of the three decks which you can then turn round. The Questioner should then put all the cards back together again in any order he or she prefers. Then you should pick up the cards so that the end that pointed towards the Questioner now points towards you. Now you are ready to begin.

5
THE CELTIC CROSS
WITH MAJOR ARCANA

There are many people who produce perfectly good readings with only Major Arcana cards. Some Readers use the Major Arcana cards from one deck in order to give an introductory reading, then give a fuller reading with a complete deck. Personally, I find the Major Arcana alone difficult to read: I prefer to 'back up' the Major cards with a couple of Minor ones.

The Celtic Cross lends itself to a Major Arcana reading because it requires only ten cards and, as there are only twenty-two Major cards to choose from, this seems a sensible way to demonstrate them at work on their own.

The Celtic Cross is probably the most frequently used spread, at least in Britain. It is described in practically every book on the Tarot and seems to be the first one that everyone learns. However, I think this is a difficult spread for a beginner to deal with and I often suggest that it is left until the student is a bit more experienced. Many people use it to give a 'blanket' reading, just to see what comes up. That idea will work well if you give the reading for someone whom you know well, because you know something of that person's circumstances and can link in to the particular aspect of their life which appears to be accented by the cards. It is not so easy to do this for a total stranger, and this leads to a certain amount of 'fishing' in order to find the particular problem or area of interest. It is, however, well suited to concentrating on one specific situation.

The Celtic Cross with Major Arcana — positions
1. The problem or circumstance surrounding the Questioner.
2. What he or she is up against.
3. The distant past.
4. The recent past, the present.
5. The near future.
6. The goal, aim or ambition of the Questioner.
7. The Questioner's feelings.
8. Outside factors.
9. The Questioner's hopes and fears.
10. The outcome.

6.

10.

9.

5.

2.

1.

4.

8.

3.

7.

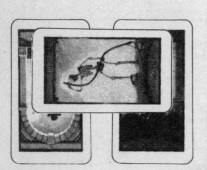

6
THE MAJOR ARCANA

The Major Arcana is so powerful in its imagery that it can be used on its own, without the Minor Arcana, even though there are only twenty-two cards. Many readers will give a Major Arcana reading followed by another reading using the whole pack. This gives them the outline of the Questioner's problems and lifestyle before going on to give the complete reading. In a mixture of Major and Minor cards, it is interesting to note how many of the Major cards appear and where.

Even though packs vary somewhat, the overall symbolism of the Major cards remains the same (i.e. the Emperor may be dressed or seated differently in different packs, but he is still the Emperor!).

There is a certain amount of controversy these days about whether to give reverse readings for cards and I believe that the majority of professional readers *do not* reverse their cards at all. The idea is that all the cards have their good and bad (weak or strong might be a better description) aspects, and this is especially true of the Major Arcana cards. I have broken the explanations down into 'positive' and 'negative' to make them a bit easier for the novice reader to understand and the 'negative' can be given as a reversed reading if so desired. Frankly, I feel that each card encompasses both sides within its nature, but I leave it to you to experiment with these cards for yourself.

O
THE FOOL

Positive
This can be shown as the first or last card in the Major Arcana. I tend to think of it as the first card as it represents a fresh start or the discovery of talents and abilities that the Questioner did not know were there. It represents a person stepping out into a new future which could take them anywhere. It is a chance to start again and it

can be applied to any aspect of life, such as a new relationship, a new area to live in, a new job, a change of direction generally. Its message is that a new door is opening and there will be challenges ahead which can be taken advantage of. The Fool can also tell of fun ahead and light hearted enjoyable people and events to come. However, even as a 'positive' card, there is a warning not to be rash, or to rush in to a new situation in a blind and undisciplined manner. Positive or negative, the Fool tells the Questioner that he is going to have to use his willpower and to exercise restraint in some future situation.

Negative
There is a clear warning here to give thought and consideration to any new situation. The Questioner will be tempted to act in an immature, possibly even irrational manner, and may become obsessed by some craze which leads them to extravagance and loss. There may be an overwhelming passion for somebody tremendously exciting, but there will be problems attached to this affair which *must* be taken into consideration before plunging in. If the warnings are ignored then at best, the outcome will make the Questioner look and feel like a prize idiot, and at worst this could be tragic.

I
THE MAGICIAN

Positive
This card depicts new opportunities, it may be the start of an enterprise or even of an important relationship, though in general, I feel that is has more to do with business matters and worldly affairs than with love and romance. There may be several courses of action to be looked at in the near future, and thought must be paid to new decisions and actions. There will soon be a chance to use skills and

education in a practical manner, but there should be some kind of politics or salesmanship involved in this somewhere.

A friend once described the Magician as indicating a 'bold step' and this is probably right as there is a somewhat chancy element attached to this card. It tells the Questioner to go ahead and blind them all with science, use the new found confidence and have a go. All in all, an important new cycle in the Questioner's life, especially that part of it which is carried on outside the home. There is definitely a feeling of the Questioner being urged to put ideas into practice because there will be great rewards for use of one's imagination, original ideas, flair, art, craft or subtlety that he or she possesses. This card could show up just as the Questioner is going to start a business using the skills and talents they possess. This is a good example because it pre-supposes self-reliance, flexibility and the ability to choose one's own action. It also shows determination to see the task through to the end.

Negative

The warning here is not to miss an opportunity that is coming up. Also to look carefully at any new enterprise which is presented to the Questioner by *other people*. They may not be all that honest. There is always an air of trickery around the Magician, either the good trickery of the successful salesman or the heartlessness of the 'cowboy' or 'con artist'. If this card depicts a person around the Questioner, he may be about to take on just the right one for the job; alternatively, the Questioner may go headlong into a business where he may find himself being controlled by a team of crooks or fools! The warning as with all the cards is that everything in life can go either way. Although consideration is essential before action when this card shows up, especially if it is upright and in a prominent part of a spread, then for goodness sake have a go!

116

II
THE HIGH PRIESTESS

Positive

If students of the occult finds this card upright and in a prominent place in the reading, then they are being told to go ahead with their studies; they *have* the ability and will make positive and helpful use of it. The Priestess has both intuition and common-sense, there is a feeling of ancient knowledge about her, about the hidden and mysterious things in life. I feel that if this card shows up when decisions are to be made, then one should follow one's feelings and let one's natural intuition be the guide, also to make allowances for somebody else's intuition particularly if they are close and trusted friends.

The Priestess also indicates scholarship in its widest sense. The card can foretell a period of study to come and of a good teacher who will be very helpful to the Questioner. It may point to a particular person about to help the Questioner, this would be a woman who is clever, rather remote but informative, if not very motherly in manner, a professionally qualified person most likely. The Questioner may take on some of the mantle of the High Priestess and find himself in a position to apple common sense and understanding. The card is also associated with integrity and honesty, so although the tongue may be sharp, the sentiments and the heart are in the right place. Of course, the Priestess, like all the cards, is somewhat androgynous, which means that 'she' may actually be a 'he'!

There is one other rather tantalizing point about the Priestess which is that it points out to the Questioner that they are not yet in possession of all the facts. The Reader must note the area of the spread in which this card falls and tell the Questioner that something pertaining to this subject has yet to be revealed.

Negative

The negative side is the opposite of cool commonsensical control, i.e. uncontrolled emotional outbursts and stupid careless remarks. Selfishness and impatience make for rows, and the Questioner is reminded to make sure that they really know what they are talking about before getting into an argument. There is a feeling of high sexual tension here as the image of the High Priestess is of an untouchable and apparently cool natured woman which makes us wonder what passions may be boiling away under her habit! However, even if uncontrolled passion is about to enter one's life, there could be something to learn, even if it is only to improve one's sexual technique!

Another aspect of this card sometimes shows up when a female Questioner is being so mindful of her family's needs that she neglects her own. She is being told not to sacrifice so much time and money on them, especially on their education, as they would learn some good practical lessons from life if she left them alone and attended to *her own* requirements a bit more.

III
THE EMPRESS

Positive

This card represents feminity in abundance, like the goddess Venus, with all her sexual charms on the one hand, and a plump loving mother caring for her children on the other. On a more down-to-earth note, there could be a child on the way when this card shows up. If the Questioner is too old to have children, this can indicate the birth of a grandchild, nephew or neice. In a man's reading, the Empress represents a warm and loving woman who makes him feel that all's right with the world. If the Questioner is thinking of getting married, then the Empress will show that the marriage will take place and be satisfying and happy. If there is nothing dramatic going on in the Questioner's love life, then this card shows that there is material satisfaction and comfort around the corner.

As a situation rather than an actual woman, the theme of fertility and abundance still counts. Like the planet Venus in astrology, the Empress is concerned with fruits of the earth, personal values and possessions, especially large and important ones. Therefore, this could show up when the Questioner is just about to move from town to country, or to buy a house with a garden. If this is the case, then the move would be beneficial. There could be more money after a pretty lean period, or just a feeling of satisfaction with oneself and one's life. A generous warm and satisfying card which is especially concerned with ownership of goods, that is of material things rather than spiritual or mental activity. The 'proprietary' feelings attached to the Empress extend to people in the sense that one says 'This is *my* child', of 'Let me introduce you to *my* wife'!

Negative
There is not much that is negative about this card but it can suggest that one is overdoing the self-indulgence bit and will regret this later. It also tends to indicate possessiveness and jealousy born of fear of rejection and loss. There is also a strong possibility of either infertility (probably temporary) or on the other hand an unwanted pregnancy. I often find that sterilization, vasectomy and abortion, or operations involving the reproductive organs, show up when this card is reversed in an important position in a spread. This does not indicate whether these situations are chosen by or forced upon the Questioner, just as the fact that they are there. There can be emotional disappointments, disenchantment with a new property, especially if it has no garden – the Empress *likes* growing things. There could be financial loss, therefore no abundance and short shrift for a time.

IIII
THE EMPEROR

Positive
The Emperor is definitely the boss! If this card represents a person who is a part of or is about to enter the Questioner's sphere of

interest, then the Questioner will definitely not be able to ignore him. This man might be a skilled business man, an elder statesman in government, or a powerful, firm but benevolent husband or father figure. If a woman is enquiring about a man she has just met and the Emperor card shows up, she can be sure that he *is* all he appears to be and will stand by her and support her. He is strong and steady by nature, with both the will and the ability to take charge in any situation. He is a good manager and reliable partner. He may not be too much fun at times, and will probably not be very talkative and entertaining, but he will stand fast and cope with any situation. Think of Jack Hawkins as the captain in 'The Cruel Sea' and you will be on the right track!

As a situation rather than a person, the Emperor represents the ability to influence people and events. The Questioner may take on some of the Emperor's personality and find him or herself moving steadily up into a position of power and influence. This indicates a firm base, a sound financial position and perhaps a secure and respected position in the community. The Questioner will be able to reach his goals and will use intelligence and reason, rather than make emotional or even intuitive judgements.

Negative
There is not much that *is* negative about this card. However, if the Questioner wants to know whether a particular person is as reliable and responsible as he seems to be, and the card comes out reversed, then I would suggest that he is not, at least for the moment, all that he is cracked up to be. This may be because he is not as strong a character as he wants others to think he is, not as reliable as the Questioner would like him to be; or is just temporarily out of stock of stiff upper lips. The reverse of the Emperor is immaturity and a lack of concentration, the inability to finish what has been started, too

much dependence upon others instead of self reliance and faith in one's own abilities. This man's apparent weakness may be due to poor health which could, of course, be a temporary situation or a sad warning that a strong and good man is not going to be able to continue with a full and active life.

V
THE HIEROPHANT

Positive
The ideas behind this card are rather difficult to put across, as the general feeling is of kindness, conformity and spiritual guidance. The Hierophant *may* turn up as a person in the Questioner's life, but this would be unusual, somehow he seems to represent situations rather than people. However, if he does, then he may literally be a teacher (especially in the sense that a Rabbi is a teacher) or even a personnel officer. He will advise the Questioner to take a good look at his motives and even to pray for guidance. When the guidance does come, it will emphasize right from wrong and will be along the lines of conventional, possibly religious thought.

As a situation, the Hierophant represents conventional behaviour. Therefore if a Questioner wants to know whether the person he or she fancies wants a conventional marriage, or prefers to live together and still go out with others, then the Hierophant, upright and in a relevant part of the spread, will definitely show that the conventional is wanted. If there is some doubt in the Questioner's mind about how to go about achieving his aims in life, the Hierophant will show that the traditional ways will lead to success. In fact tradition, spirituality and following the dictates of God, one's conscience and the tried and tested methods of working and living are going to be the most successful in this case. There will be kindness and help from people around the Questioner. The older, more staid people will be the ones to offer useful advice and help. If this card shows up when the Questioner's affairs are being held up, it signifies that the delay will not be for much longer.

Negative

There really is not much that is negative about this card except to say that the Questioner may be his own worst enemy by being too timid and too aware of other people's requirements while neglecting his own. It is strange that the two cards who represent people who train and teach us (the Hierophant and the High Priestess) should also warn against being *too* kind-hearted. They are telling us that making excuses for other people's weaknesses is not going to do anyone any good and a dose of firmness may be of more benefit in the long run to all concerned. It is better to stand up for yourself when you know you are right. The other problems are of hypocrisy and self doubt. Be honest, at least with yourself, *that* is the message here.

When the Hierophant is reversed, then non-conformity will be the order of the day. For instance, if the Questioner wants to know whether the person they are interested in desires marriage, then the answer will be negative. There is also the feeling that a more relaxed attitude to matters of business may be more productive, therefore, the Questioner would be better not to put things on a firm traditional footing, but just let things slide along for a while and see what turns up. In others words, do not try to coerce someone into marraige, or into strict modes of operating which will not suit. The Questioner should be prepared to accept novel ways of thinking and not be captive to their own ideas or too full of their own opinions.

VI
THE LOVERS

Positive

There are two distinct and very different messages from this card. On the one hand it can mean exactly what it looks like, i.e. that love, romance and passion are coming to the Questioner. In this context it means that a relationship is just around the corner or one which is worrying the Questioner will bloom into love and marriage. On a milder note this card means friendship and harmony. Therefore, if it shows up in an area relating to work, it would mean that relationships

with colleagues at work or with business partners will be happy and productive. As well as meaning attraction, this card is often interpreted as beauty. When one finds someone attractive, they become beautiful even if they are, strictly speaking, not good looking. If there has been a parting, for whatever reason, the Lovers card indicates that the partners will soon be reunited.

The other meaning attached to the Lovers is of *choice*. This means that the Questioner is soon going to have to choose between two people, two courses of action, two jobs or two of anything, and that the matter of choosing is going to be very important in its outcome. The obvious impression is of choosing between sacred and profane love, and this may well be the case; but the general idea is that the choice has some sort of right or wrong influence, selfish or unselfish, easy or tough. A common matter of choice for women these days is whether to have a career, or opt for an old fashioned family life.

Negative
When the Lover appears reversed, it can mean a temporary or permanent parting, the end of a relationship rather than the beginning, but this will be made clearer by reference to the rest of the reading. It also warns of making a mistake, tying oneself up with the wrong person or for the wrong reasons. The Questioner will remain frustrated in their desires (carnal or otherwise) if they do not make an effort or make their feelings a bit more obvious to the other person. Another problem is infatuation, wanting someone who is clearly wrong for all concerned.

VII
THE CHARIOT

Positive

The Chariot is associated with a time of hard work and major effort, and it is often retro-active, which means that it is just as likely to show the phase which has recently passed by as to indicate something which has yet to come. Either way, it is associated with a struggle, and a time when one does not know whether one is on one's head or one's heels. There could be a great ordeal here, a time of strain and overwork but the feeling is that the outcome makes all the effort worthwhile. This may be a course of action which is deliberately chosen by the Questioner like going into business or moving house, thereby incurring a lot of work in getting the project off the ground. The troubles may, of course, be something not of the Questioner's choosing, which would mean dealing with a knotty problem which is definitely going to need hard work, patience and endurance to solve. The feeling is that a victory is achieved here despite setbacks. In a way it is quite a simple card to interpret, because it means that things have been, still are, or about to be, very hard to handle for a while – but that the outcome is good. The general feeling of the Chariot is of purposeful activity.

On a more practical note, this card often shows up when the Questioner is about to buy a new vehicle, or to have one MoT'd or set to rights, in this case it is a good omen. The Chariot may also indicate that the Questioner will be travelling soon, possibly in connection with work. I have noticed that vehicles – planes, boats, even bicycles – enter the life of the Questioner after this card turns up in a spread.

Negative

The meaning here is much the same as above, but the Questioner has less chance of winning outright, or the struggle is going against them at the moment. This does not mean that it will always be that way, things may change. The one sure thing about the Chariot is that it shows a time of tension and hard work which cannot and will not go on forever. If this card *is* reversed, then the problems are more likely to have been presented *to*, rather than chosen *by*, the Questioner. This card sometimes predicts problems with regard to vehicles.

VIII
JUSTICE

Positive

The meaning of this card is actually quite obvious – it represents justice, fairness, balance, etc. This card often comes up when there are legal matters to be dealt with, and on the whole it can be taken to mean that the outcome will be good. If the card shows up *reversed* in the ninth position in an Astrological spread (see page 147), it would not be good news legally.

The Justice card does not restrict itself strictly to legal matters, it encompasses all matters relating to fairness and justice in the wider sense. For instance, this would be a terrific card to have if a partnership or joint venture is about to be entered. Although it is stretching things somewhat, even a forthcoming marriage could show up with this card, as it would show that the union would bring harmony and a feeling of completeness and balance to the couple involved. If the Questioner is involved in any kind of argument, or has been in any way accused of doing something wrong, he will soon be proved right. There could be agreements through discussion, or a situation where the Questioner acts in an honest manner when others around them do not and this honesty, loyalty and idealism are shown to be right.

Negative
This is one of those cards which does need some extra consideration if it comes out reversed, as it does appear to reverse the meaning of the upright version. That is to say, legal problems will continue or will not be resolved to the Questioner's satisfaction. If there are no legal matters concerning the Questioner, then he or she is being warned of some sort of unfair treatment or unfair accusation to come. There could be a lack of promotion, or some other setback due to somebody who is engaging in underhand politics. The Questioner may have to apologise to someone or make a special effort to keep the peace.

VIIII
THE HERMIT

Positive
This is not an easy card to interpret as its meaning is subtle, it also tends to give advice to the Questioner rather than show a forthcoming event. It indicates that the Questioner will need to take some time out to think things over.

There could be an important decision to make, or just one of those times when there will be a need for reflection and consideration of long term aims and ambitions. This may show that the Questioner would benefit from the advice of an expert, or just a sensible and sympathetic friend. He or she could do well to withdraw from active life for a while in order to meditate, pray and give some thought to the larger issues of life and death. There is another meaning to this card and that means that the Questioner will need to be cautious and prudent in some forthcoming situation. This card contains an element of self denial, and it all fits in with the idea of living quietly for a while, possibly doing without something or someone. It can mean a time of loneliness ahead, which may be self-imposed. There could even be a time of convalescence. The retreat from life and company may be self-imposed or imposed from outside, but it will be beneficial if the Questioner makes the most of the peaceful and reflective period.

Negative

In my experience there are two or three meanings to this. Firstly, there may be a petulant refusal of help in a difficult situation. The Questioner could turn away from family or friends, and cut his nose to spite his face.

Secondly, there could be a failure to grow up and see things as they really are. Both of these are the kind of state of mind which results from a person being hurt or rejected in some way, jealousy or fear are likely to be at the back of this behaviour.

The third ideas is that the Questioner might be left alone, bereaved or let down by a lover or partner and may feel very lonely, rejected and down-hearted for a while. Sometimes the questioner, 'Is he coming back?' is answered by a reversed Hermit (plus other pointers) as being 'no'.

X
WHEEL OF FORTUNE

Positive

Whenever the Wheel of Fortune appears in a spread it signifies change. The Questioner is being told that nothing stays the same forever, and in this particular case changes are definitely on the way. It would be nice to suggest that the changes are for the better, but this is not necessarily so. Just think of a ferris wheel in a fairgound, the little seats with their cargo of laughing passengers are travelling *up* on one side of the wheel, at the same time others are travelling *down* on the other side. Therefore let us be optimists and suggest that the Wheel indicates a turn for the better, a chance coming from out of the blue, a stroke of luck, great opportunity or even a godsend. Certainly this card shows that events related to the sphere of life it represents in the spread are going to be changing.

Most Readers like to see this as an optimistic card, but it may not be so – the best that one can say is that any sudden setbacks can be viewed as a challenge which give the Questioner a chance to grow in whatever area of life is affected by the changes to come. The *placement* of this card in a spread is actually more important than the card itself as it is meant to show *where* the greatest changes will come.

Negative

There really isn't a reverse meaning for this card except that if the upright Wheel can be taken to represent an upturn in fortunes, then the reversed Wheel may bring unexpected setbacks. This may herald the end of a rather easy phase and the beginning of a stressful time to come. There are challenges here and the Questioner will be given the chance to rise to the occasion or let himself become downhearted.

XI
STRENGTH

Positive

On a very simple and straightforward level this card shows that somebody who has been ill is going to recover soon. If the person indicated in the spread has been feeling tired, down-hearted or has just not been coping with things too well lately, then things are bound to improve.

On another level, this card shows that the Questioner will be able to overcome future obstacles, have the courage and resolution to cope. There will be calm perseverence and determination, especially when under pressure. Plans may be put into action soon, achievements and success lie ahead. This is a good card to have when interviews and exams are due.

Above all, the mood of the Strength card is of quiet courage of the unspectacular kind in the face of long term challenges. Conscience will be the guide and the forces of truth and light will triumph over spiteful and jealous behaviour. Ignorance and oppression will be overcome, goodwill will win over evil intentions.

Negative

This shows that the Questioner, or the relevant person in their environment, is not yet well. It is a warning of continued health problems, or that someone is drained of energy and hope.

There is also the possibility that a struggle will be just too much and that an enemy will gain ascendency over the Questioner. There may have to be a postponement or abandonment of plans soon. There is a lack of courage and resolution and the Questioner is warned that underhanded behaviour will land them in trouble.

XII
THE HANGED MAN

Positive

This card represents a suspension in affairs which will be followed by a turning point in the Questioner's life. However, the changes are more likely to be in *mental attitude* rather than in actual events – although events could conspire to cause this. The general impression is that the Questioner will soon abandon outmoded methods of thought in favour of a more philosophical outlook on life. The effect of this card is often descirbed as taking someone away from materialism towards a more spiritual outlook on life. This concept involves sacrifice in some form or other. A good illustration of this idea carried out to the ultimate, would be that of St Francis of Assisi who gave up a comfortable life for something which seemed to make more sense to him.

This card may show up when a destructive relationship is coming to an end, and it shows the Questioner that, although they may be lonely (i.e. suspended) for a while, it really will be for the best in the long run. If there are financial or other losses, then the Questioner is being told that they will 'grow' in character as a result of dealing with these problems, and that perhaps this is needed in order to make somebody more appreciative of the non-material aspects of life such as love, friendship or self respect. One simple instance of this kind of gradual change in circumstances is when loving parents find that their brood is leaving the nest.

On a practical level this card says that there may be something very good which results from difficult circumstances, such as the Questioner being given the sack from his job, a situation which will require the Questioner to assess his or her abilities and could, when seen in the long run, be very beneficial. There will definitely be some form of hiatus between the former situation and what is yet to come, there must be some sacrifices made, this should be used constructively so as to create a satisfactory future outlook on life.

Negative

There is not much that *is* negative about this card except that it advises the Questioner to take a philosophical view of any sacrifices that he or she may have to make. It also shows that the Questioner may be longing for change and not able to accept the rather stagnant situation that is going to prevail over the next few months. This card shows the need to grow up and accept that situations are not always of one's own choosing but occasionally have to be endured for a while.

There is a warning against making *useless* sacrifices, or putting up with a poor situation because it is easier and less frightening than taking the risk of making changes. The Questioner should stop banging his or her head against the same old brick wall. Clear and objective thought is required now, seek guidance, then take the road which feels right inside.

XIII
DEATH

Positive

This card usually puts the wind up people when it appears in a spread, but I have *never* known it to mean that the Questioner is about to die! To be honest, in certain circumstances I *have* seen this card foretell the death of somebody in the life of the Questioner, but this is usually no great surprise as the dying person is generally old and very sick by the time of the reading.

The more usual meaning of this card is *change*. This means that the Questioner can expect some situation to come to a complete end which clears the way for a fresh start. An apparent misfortune may be a blessing in disguise. There may be death of the old self, inner or outer changes that will lead shortly to a new way of life. On the whole, I would suggest that the events which cause changes are not going to be pleasant to begin with, there may be the loss of a friendship or relationship of long standing. Somebody may leave, there may be financial losses or, in extreme circumstances, the loss of a home or a change in one's health (look at other cards for some sort of indication). However, the meaning here is that there is always a chance to make good. Changes which may be hard to cope with will clear away a certain amount of unnecessary rubbish from the past and leave the Questioner free to make a new start.

Negative
There is really no different from the 'positive' reading except that on the one hand the effects should not be quite so drastic or so out of the blue. There is a warning that this situation should be dealt with in a fairly positive and active manner or a terrible feeling of lethargy and depression might set in. This card also indicates that the Questioner may be stagnating, afraid of losing what he now has.

XIIII
TEMPERANCE

Positive
This is a very pleasant card, it foretells a time of peace and harmony to come. If the Questioner has been going through a rather fraught period, he will soon be feeling calmer and coping better. In fact, the central impression of the Temperance card is of coping well and relaxing. There is harmony here, this may be applied to future relationships, family situations, work, money, health, in fact any aspect of life. The position of this card in a spread will give the Reader an idea of how to interpret this.

The other theme of this card is that of *moderation*. Therefore, if the Questioner has been overdoing anything, be it work or play, good sense and a balanced attitude will apply in the future. There may be a time of frugality when this card appears, this should not be too much of a struggle as it will give the Questioner a chance to make good use of what he already has. There may be some slight material hardships, but spirituality will bring comfort. To my mind this card says, 'Put your feet up, you've done enough'.

Negative

The only negative ideas that this card suggests are that the Questioner will be too busy in the future to be able to see where he is really going. There may be continued pressures and anxieties and the Questioner may find it difficult to cope with all the separate demands that there are on his or her time. Frankly, the answer here is to make an assessment of what can be left for another time and to concentrate on what absolutely must be done.

Intemperance is also a possibility, so if the Questioner is overdoing the good things of life, the advice is to cut back a bit.

XV
THE DEVIL

Positive

This is the card which upsets people who are religious or are afraid of Tarot cards in general because we all know that the Devil is evil. Well, so he is, but the evil can be of our making in that we allow ourselves to behave stupidly. There is a strong warning here not to be talked into evil (or even black magic) by dangerous people. There is also an element of bondage; enslavement to outmoded ideas possibly, or to a job or house which needs to be left for good. The most obvious form of slavery comes from being tied to people who are no good for you. Perhaps it is time to take a realistic look at current relationships and to stop blaming others without also looking inwardly. The Devil urges the Questioner to be very practical, even with essentially non-practical matters.

The Questioner needs to become more independent and to stop accepting unpleasant situations just for the sake of peace. The message here is that one will continue to be oppressed unless the chains are broken. If this card shows up in an area concerned with money, then it might show that for the time being, the Questioner will be tied to a particular job because he or she cannot afford to do otherwise. Perhaps there is a way out, it is possible to gain qualifications and become trained for something better, even though it might take a long time. It is worth thinking positively and practically about future improvements and changes. Above all, the Devil is a practical lad, not spiritual at all!

This card is also concerned with sexual matters. There are many reasons why sex could present problems, but the message of this card is that sex may well become an important factor in any future decisions. Also that the Questioner may soon be involved in an extremely hot and passionate love affair.

Negative
Frankly, this card is fairly negative whichever way up it is, but the reverse meaning can show that the influence is passing, and that the chains which have held the Questioner are shortly going to be broken. The Questioner is beginning to wake up about the situation and may shortly be able to do something really positive to break out.

This card still warns of becoming involved with evil people and of dirty deeds to come. Follow your conscience, take good advice and when in doubt, keep to the straight and narrow.

XVI
THE TOWER

Positive
This is a most unpleasant card to find in a reading. To be honest, I advise people not to get *too* worried unless it comes up in repeated

readings, but whatever way one cares to look at it the Tower brings bad news. There is definitely going to be some sort of loss, even a calamity of some kind. Security, as the Questioner has known it in the past, is going to be destroyed and the troubles are likely to come amazingly quickly when they start. Illusions are going to be shattered and the truth about people and situations will be revealed in startling clarity. There will be a questioning of previously accepted beliefs, trust will be destroyed. There could even be some sort of disgrace.

I am by nature an optimist, but even I cannot find much that is good about this card. At one time I kept getting the Tower in my own readings, and sure enough, our family suffered an appalling financial loss, but we fought our way back to solvency and feel quite proud of ourselves having done so.

Negative

Negative and positive are not really apt terms for this card; however, to see this card reversed in a spread does seem to show that the problems are here and now rather than in the future. The reversed Tower indicates something in the nature of a long term misery, rather than a sudden catastrophe, although current and future difficulties may be stemming from a sudden disaster in the recent past. Also, the Questioner can now either make strides to overcome difficult circumstances or remain in the midst of them. There is likely to be continued oppression, the problems are not solved yet.

XVII
THE STAR

Positive

This card is truly the 'Star of Hope'. amd it brings hope, faith and optimism to any part of the spread that it touches. In general, it is a clear indication that things will go well in the future. If the Questioner has been going through a particularly rough patch, then life will soon become smooth again. If there has been a health problem, then this is a wonderful card to see in a reading.

On a more practical note, it is worth taking account of the position of the Star in a spread as its message may apply to a particular area of life. For instance, if applied to career matters, it could show that a problem will soon be solved, past efforts will be appreciated and rewarded. New enterprises or new jobs will go well, promotion could be on the way and any new venture will flourish. Obviously, this hopeful message can be applied to relationships, exam prospects – even the driving test. If it seems to show up in a relatively unimportant area of the spread, such as a holiday, then it would be telling the Reader that this particular holiday is going to be a good deal more for the Questioner than they imagine.

There is something of an educational slant to this card as it can mean that educational and artistic matters are soon going to be important and that the Questioner would soon be able to make good use of his or her talents. Travel could be on the way, because the general idea of this card is expansion of the horizons and very positive new experiences. It sometimes indicates an increasing and purely beneficial interest in the occult.

Negative

This card does not really have a negative side to it except that it can show some doubts about a new venture, there is a touch of pessimism when the Star is reversed, and perhaps a warning not to expand one's horizons too much just at the moment. It just shows some doubt about the future.

XVIII
THE MOON

Positive

The central theme of this card is one of illusion. This is rather a difficult concept to understand as mystery and illusion can be both good and bad depending on the nature of the Questioner and the area of life that this card affects. Experience has taught me that if this

card pops up early on in a Tarot session, then I am dealing with highly charged emotions. If the Questioner has just fallen in love and is not sure how things are going, if a relationship seems to be going nowhere, or working its way to a close, then the Moon will often be one of the first cards to appear. This card clearly shows that everybody concerned in the relationship is muddled, not sure about what they want or where they are going. There could be a good deal of insincerity on both sides. There is no sensible advice that a Reader can hope to give as these kinds of problems defy logic. The Questioner's best hope is to avoid making too many concrete plans and let things float along for a while.

If the Moon card points to other areas of life, such as finances or work, then deception and trickery are definitely in the air. On a very mundane level, even simple plans can be screwed up when the Moon arrives on the scene, letters will go awry, travel plans will be completely fouled up. Messes, muddles, deception, lies and frustration are on the way for sure, and if there is a woman around who can give the Questioner trouble, she will not hesitate to do so.

On a more positive side, the Moon gives the Questioner a chance to use his or her imagination, and this can be positively channelled into artistic pursuits. There could soon be a development of occult powers. The Questioner would do well to rely on 'gut feelings' in relation to any doubtful situations, as they are going to be far more accurate than reason.

Negative
This card is much the same either way up, but lies and insincerity will definitely be around the Questioner, the muddles and failures may be of a fairly minor matter, but they will be irritating just the same. Either way up, this annoying card can tease the poor Questioner by showing that the future is yet to be revealed and that the cards are not

in the mood to be particularly informative just now.

XVIIII
THE SUN

Positive

This is a lovely card, as it means joy and happiness are on the way. The sun is about to shine on the Questioner and will soon make him feel very good. There is not much to say about this card except that whatever area of the Questioner's life is touched by it will bring happiness and success. If there has been poor health, then there could be no better card to turn up. All efforts will be rewarded, trials overcome, there will be good friends, comfort and happiness. Marriage will be happy and successful, there will be unselfish love and a great deal of fun and frolic ahead. All proposed enterprises will go well.

I have often seen this card show up shortly before the birth of a child, and if the Questioner is doubtful about the ability to have children, then there could be no better card to find than the Sun. There may be grandchildren soon, or just neighbourhood children, the Questioner may even be working among children, but whatever the connection, there will be joy and fun of a youthful and exuberant nature.

Negative

This shows that there is *potential* for happiness ahead but that it is rather clouded at the moment. There will be success and achievement, but it may take a bit of time to come along. There will be great improvements but complete satisfaction will take a little longer to achieve.

This card can sometimes be a little sad when associated with children. It may show that a child is shortly to become sick, or that there may be difficulties related to pregnancy or birth. It is even possible, when looked at with other cards in the spread, that a child could prove to be a nuisance in the eyes of the Questioner, or the cause of disagreements. The reversed Sun sometimes shows up when the Questioner decides against having a child and can indicate a forthcoming sterilization, vasectomy or even an abortion (especially if the reversed Empress is also in the spread).

This card also indicates that the Questioner's marriage is not a great success and that he or she is not appreciated.

XX
JUDGEMENT

Positive

This card indicates that a phase is definitely coming to an end. The Questioner will soon be able to look back over what they have been doing and make a clear evaluation of past events. In practical terms, the Judgement card could mean rewards, promotions or even a retirement party with gifts and good wishes for the future. Although this card represents an ending, it is more of a logical conclusion than a wrench, and in any circumstances the Questioner will feel that he has done his duty and now has a clear conscience.

All endings are also beginnings, the end of a project also means the chance to start a new one, and at least the Questioner will start out with the confidence of having accomplished the previous project satisfactorily. There is a feeling of rejuvenation attached to this card, therefore if one has been tied down looking after a sick or demanding relative who is possibly soon to be released from suffering, then the

Questioner will feel satisfied that they have done all that could be done and at the same time will also relish the freedom of being able to make a fresh and unfettered start.

There is another far more practical level to this card, and that is of strictly *legal* judgments. If the Questioner is due to have any dealings with the law, then the outcome will be favourable. I suppose it is not surprising but I often find this card turning up when the Questioner is on the point of a divorce as, on the one hand, it shows the end of the marriage and on the other, the legal settlements which are to come.

Negative
The reversed Judgment card still refers to endings but the feeling is that the Questioner will not be too satisfied with the circumstances surrounding the events. This could mean that the Questioner would know in his heart of hearts that he could have done much better. That could apply to educational matters, work or relationships. The Questioner knows that they could have been a better friend, or just done more for others. There has been a shortsighted and selfish attitude somewhere along the line.

On another level, legal matters are not well starred when this card turns up reversed – especially in any position in a spread which refers specifically to the law.

XXI
THE WORLD

Positive
If the Questioner is nearing the end of a project, then he will soon be able to survey the work done with a sense of pride and accomplishment.

This card, like so many of the Major Arcana, is about turning points but in this case a gradual and satisfactory ending with the implicit feeling that new projects soon to be embarked upon will go well too. There is success on the way, there will be praise and reward for satisfactory completion. The Questioner will elicit the admiration of others and will have reason to feel proud. There will be good fortune and above all spiritual enlightenment. The World card shows clearly that the Questioner is about to gain some insight and a sense of inner peace.

On a more mundane level, this card often indicates travel and can even go as far as to suggest emigration because it carries the notion of a new life in a new place. This may just be a move of house, particularly if it is in connection with a change in the Questioner's circumstances, for example, children being born or becoming independent. But in my experience there is more than a hint of foreign places and of new adventures to come.

Negative
The Questioner might display an ability to accept change and an unreasonable desire to stick in a rut, but on the other hand, this could be a good thing as it shows stability and permanence rather than uncertainty and restlessness.

The worst aspect of the negative World is that the Questioner may find himself envious of other people and unsatisfied with his own progress. However, all is not lost even now, there can be fulfilled ambitions and a fair amount of success, but only after a bit of trime has passed. Be patient, keep trying, that is the message here.

PART THREE

FORTUNE-TELLING

with

DICE

7
SYMBOLS

RED DICE – SIX SPOTS – BAT

'For the black bat, night, has flown' – just one line from *'Maud'* by Alfred, Lord Tennyson which shows quite clearly one view of this creature – something black and usually evil, a creature of the night and darkness, transitory – of a passing nature. In medieval Europe it was linked with death and witchcraft and thought to fly with its head down because its brain is heavy. Its wings were also looked on as an infernal attribute.

In China, however, the bat was associated with happiness and long life as it supposedly lived to be a thousand. Bat talismans were worn to promote longevity. They were often made in the form of five bats linked together when they stood for luck, wealth, longevity, health and peace – 'that which all men desire'. Occasionally only two bats were depicted to symbolize good wishes. This two-bat talisman was a favourite gift between friends. To the Japanese they symbolized happiness and prosperity and were called komori.

There is a tenuous link between the bat and the Hanged Man in Tarot, as they are both symbolic of inversion – they are both objects which are depicted upside-down. The bat is symbolic of shadow. Just as the sun represents the light side of the spirit, the bat, in its role of shadow, is the negative 'double' of the body – the image of its evil and base side. Primitive people regarded shadow as the soul, or 'alter ego' – a belief which is echoed in the literature and folktales of some advanced cultures. Jung used the term 'shadow' to mean the primitive and instinctive side of an individual.

In Finno-Ugric a bat was believed to be one of the forms the soul can take during sleep, and for this reason it was not seen during the day when people are awake. In Bohemia, to carry the right eye of a bat was thought to bring invisibility.

Key Words and Phrases: a passing shadow which can hide good and evil, warning, danger signal, omen, prediction, prophecy.

Subsidiary meanings:

Passing – course of time, matter of time, process of time, lapse of time, march of time, duration, progress, flow, run, roll, proceed, advance, run its course, expire, end, go by, pass by, enjoy a spell, in due time, fullness of time, with the days, approach towards, in transit.

Shadow – dream, ghost, illusion, smokescreen, cloak, blanket, veil, cover, darken, cloud, fog, mist, glaze, make opaque, obscure, blur, overcast, vague, undefined, confused, indistinct, conceal, loom, cover.

Hide – conceal, camouflage, disguise, smoke-screen, mystify, suppress, unintelligible, mask, confine, keep in, lock up, seclude, seal up, bottle up, cover over, gloss over, stifle, smother, keep back, reserve, withhold.

Good – blessing in disguise, for the best, to one's advantage, luck, windfall, favourable, happy, prosperous.

Evil – mischieviousness, foul play, to one's cost, nuisance, annoying, harm, damage, injurious, troubles, troublesome.

Danger Signal – warning, alarm-bell, alert, omen, prediction, prophecy, forwarned, distress signal, alert, arouse, frighten, startle.

RED DICE – FIVE SPOTS – BEETLE

The beetle, and in particular the Egyptian scarab, is one of the most common of all magical charms, probably because of its symbolic link with the sun. The Egyptians regarded the beetle, pushing its egg-containing ball of dung across the ground, as an earthly equivalent of the sun, that great ball of light which appears to be rolled across the sky. It also symbolizes the hope of a life hereafter.

The Egyptian scarab beetle, like the crab, has as its function the attribute of devouring what is transitory – the volatile element in alchemy – and of contributing to moral and physical regeneration. It is interesting to note that scarab is the word source of both crab and scar.

The beetle is a vital component of a South American Indian legend. They believed that this creature created the world and from the grains of earth he had left over he fashioned man and woman. The Ancient Hebrews, like the Egyptians, believed that the beetle procreated as it walked backwards towards the west, the region of darkness, and it became symbolic of darkness, obscurity and shadows.

Key Words and Phrases: doggedness, determination, single-mindedness, purposefulness, specific ambition, targets.

Subsidiary meanings:

Doggedness – perseverance, persistence, tenacity, stubbornness, obstinacy, steadfastness, resolution, concentration, application, tirelessness, plodding on, endurance, patience, repeated efforts, staying power, a trier, a stayer, indomitable, keep at it, never take 'no' for an answer, never despair, never say die, have what it takes, unfailing, try, try and try again, continue, keep going, work till one drops, hang on.

Determination – fixity of purpose, compulsion, unbending, intent upon, serious, devoted, dedicated, see it through, take the plunge.

Specific Ambition – chosen, special, named, decided upon, purpose, resolve, pursuit, in mind, future intention, desire, ultimate goal, target, desired object, project, scheme, something to aim at.

RED DICE – FOUR SPOTS – HORSESHOE

The horseshoe is a universal symbol of good luck. This luck has been attributed for a number of reasons. Firstly, horseshoes are made from iron, the magic metal which is supposed to drive away witches and evil spirits. They are fashioned by blacksmiths, workers with fire and iron, who for centuries were believed to have special powers. Also, they are closely connected with the horse, a sacred beast in many cultures, symbolic of virility and fertility and ridden by heroes and gods. Finally, they resemble, in shape, the crescent moon, symbol of Isis.

Horseshoes were especially lucky if they were found on the road where a horse had cast them. The usual practice was to take the shoe home and nail it over the front door or threshold. Care

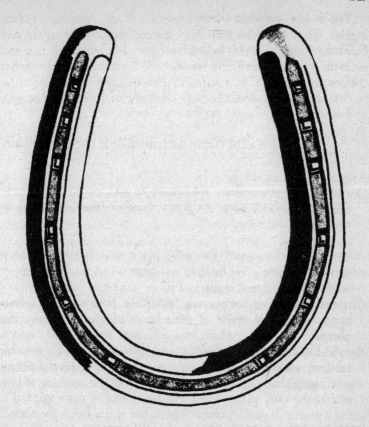

had to be taken, however, to ensure that the horseshoe was hung the correct way up. The points had to face upwards so that the good luck would not drain away. Another belief was that bad luck was trapped in the circle and because the devil cannot cross the opening he would keep running backwards and forwards inside. The luckiest horseshoes to find have four nails on one side and only three on the other which totals seven, a number which is believed to be extremely fortunate. If a young girl found a horseshoe the nails left on it were said to number the years before she would marry.

Christian and pagan beliefs often became interwoven in many old superstitions. The following charm, which should be recited aloud while nailing a horseshoe over the door, is one such example:

Father, Son and Holy Ghost,
Nail the devil to this post,
Thrice I smite with Holy Crook,
With this mell I thrice do knock,
One for God,
And one for Wod(en),
And one for Lok(i), (or maybe even 'luck').

In Shropshire, instead of taking the horseshoe home another ritual
was used:

Pick'en up'e'orse's shoe, and spatter en wi' spittle. Mak' a wish
fully quickly and throw en o'er't shooter (shoulder), walk by
an' ne'er glance'e back.

Above a door was not the only place that horseshoes were
nailed to promote good luck. It was quite a common sight to see
horseshoes nailed to the sides of mine workings in this country.
Along the east coast, particularly in Suffolk, fishermen would nail
a horseshoe to the masts of their boats to protect them from
shipwreck, a practice which was followed by Admiral Nelson,
who had one nailed to the mainmast of his ship. Even the humble
horseshoe nail was deemed to have magical properties and people
would carry them in their pockets to keep rheumatism at bay.
China is the only place where the horseshoe is not regarded as
being a source of good fortune. There, the entire hoof of a horse is
looked upon as a symbol of good luck.

In the Middle Ages the combination of ash tree wood and
horseshoe was an important medicinal charm. The practice was to
bury a shoe in the roots of the tree. Sometimes it was hung on an
ash bough so that the branches would eventually grow round it.
Twigs from an ash tree, which had been treated in this fashion,
were brushed over the backs of sick cattle to cure them of their
ailments.

Key Words and Phrases: good fortune, happiness, laughter,
good luck especially in a gamble, successful plans.

Subsidiary meanings:
Good Luck/Good Fortune – prosperity, well-being, hapiness, health
and wealth, success, have all the luck, crest of the wave,

affluence, plenty, luxury, golden touch, Midas touch, fat of the land, smile of fortune, blessings, luck, prestige, bed of roses, halcyon days, thriving, up and coming, fortunate, make hay, fall on one's feet, turn out well, run of luck, on a good thing.

Happiness – joy, pleasure, enjoyment, pleasant times, merry, blissful, have the pleasure, pleased, delight in, relish, have fun.

Laughter – rejoicing, thanksgiving, be joyful, celebrate, let yourself go, make merry, flash a smile, loosen up, unwind, fun and games.

Gamble – risk-taking, plunge, risk, hazard, speculate, flutter, leap in the dark, have a go, experiment, chance, venture, try your luck, risk it.

Successful – happy ending, favourable issue, time well spent, breakthrough, achieve, accomplish, triumph, win, effective, profitable, foolproof, make the grade, arrive, show results, bear fruit, do the trick.

Plans – intentions, calculations, future pursuits, projects, designs, schemes, proposals, objects, ends, have every intention, aim at, strive after, heart set upon, promise oneself, aspire to, dream of, eye upon.

RED DICE – THREE SPOTS – BOAT

A wet sheet and a flowing sea,
 A wind that follows fast
And fills the white and rustling sail
 And bends the gallant mast;
And bends the gallant mast, my boys,
 While like the eagle free
Away the good ship flies, and leaves
 Old England on the lee.

—A. Cunningham.

Stirring lines – and what a picture they evoke of excitement, travel and adventure with a great sailing vessel outward bound in search of new lands and new routes between distant peoples. The boat has been replaced by a boot on modern dice and, although some of the imagery has been lost, the interpretation remains the same.

Boat and ship are synonymous and in Christian symbolism the ship represents the Christian church. In the most general sense boats represent 'a vehicle' and the opportunity for travel and

discovery. Before the advent of 'air mail' letters from overseas were carried by sea and the boat has become linked with news from a distance – messages and communications.

The ship has often been described as the Solar Boat (life) making its voyage across the Ocean – a symbol of the unconscious and darkness. And the ship of death is the means by which the body is carried from one life to the next. Life, when represented as a boat, can be steered and the most profound significance of navigation is that implied by Pompey the Great when he said – 'Living is not necessary, but navigation is.'

Key Words and Phrases: travel, outward journeys, expeditions, quests, searches, movement, messages and communications.

Subsidiary meanings:

Travel – successive change of place, make journeys, movement, going, march on, motion towards, move, go, make your way, remove, change places, set going.

Outward Journeys – projection, outgoing, outward bound, departure, exodus, travel, itinerancy, globe-trotting, tourism, voyage, passage, trip, expedition, course, trek, business trip, errand, progress, tour, jaunt, joy ride, outing, excursion, wanderlust, rambling, stopping-over, visiting, nomadic, migratory, footloose, see the world, explore, go places, sightsee, go forth, take wing, wend one's way, gad about.

Quests/Searches – pursuit, enterprise, hunt, search-party, in quest of, sent after, in pursuit, in full cry, on the trail, seek, look for, cast about, follow the scent, track, be after, aim at, intend, undertaking, obligation, labour of love, adventure, probe, treasure-hunt, enquire, question, ransack, rummage, comb, go through, grope for, seek a clue.

Movement – motivation, coming and going, hive of industry, plenty to do, pressure of work, things going on, restlessness, energy, activity, bustle, eventful, hard at it.

Messages/Communications – notification, bulletin, announcement, declaration, news, report, information, tidings, word of mouth, cable, telegram, letter, postcard, telephone, signal, intelligence.

RED DICE – TWO SPOTS – SKULL

Behold this ruin! 'Twas a skull
Once of ethereal spirit full!
This narrow cell was Life's retreat;
This place was Thought's mysterious seat!
What beauteous pictures fill'd that spot,
What dreams of pleasure, long forgot!
Nor Love, nor Joy, nor Hope, nor Fear,
Has left one trace, one record here.

Lines to a skull – Anna Jane Vardill – 1816

The skull is not the most pleasant of symbols and is a constant reminder to man of his own mortality. It represents death, transitoriness and the vanity of earthly life. The skull, like a snail's shell, is what survives the living once the body has gone forever. For this reason it becomes significant as a receptacle of life and thought. Leblant describes the skull as 'the semi-spherical crown of the human body' which signifies the heavens, whilst Plato in *Timaeus* declares that 'the human head is the image of the world.'

Skulls were once objects employed in divination. The origin of the belief in a head discoursing after death probably has its roots in such legends as Arthur, Bran, Mimir and Orpheus. This idea can also be found in Shakespeare's *Hamlet*. In Norse mythology it was believed that the heavens were made from the skull of Ymir, a primaeval giant.

Key Words and Phrases: mortality, death, change by transformation, sudden unexpected change, alterations, new situations.

Subsidiary meanings:

Mortality – impermanence, brittleness, fragility, briefness, time-bound, passing, for the moment, here today gone tomorrow.

Death – extinction, destruction, abolition, end of, finish, cancellation, wipe clean, vanished, no more, obsolete, over and done with, pass away, leave no trace, cancel, abolish, wipe out.

Transformation – alteration, variation, difference, adjust, swap, improvement, convert, adapt, revise, reform, unrecognizable, change the form, appearance or character of, alter out of all recognition.

Sudden/Unexpected – unprepared, surprise, shock, jolt, bolt from the blue, bombshell, eye-opener, revelation, amazing, unguessed, unforseen, not-anticipated, unannounced, improbable, not bargained for, unaccountable, taken aback, caught napping, sprung on, bowl over, without notice.

New Situations – not previously in existence, modern, recent, unheard of, up to date, revolutionary, move with the times, circumstances, environment, look of things, lay of the land, positions, settings, locations, directions, bearings, job, station, predicament.

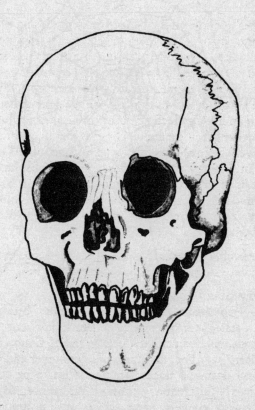

RED DICE – ONE SPOT – WEB

The web of our life is of a mingled yarn, good and ill together.

All's Well That Ends Well – Shakespeare.

As a symbol the web needs little explanation – it represents just what it is – a trap, an illusion and a source of danger to the unwary. Symbolically the web and the spider are closely linked – one is the trap, the other the trapper. The Mayans regarded the spider as the eternal weaver of the web of illusion. They also believed that death wound up the thread of an old life in order to spin a new one.

The web can be viewed not only as a symbol of life, destiny and fate but also as a spiral net converging to a central point – the centre of the world.

The last words on the subject should come from Scott. In his poem *Marmion* he sums up the whole concept in just two lines:

O what a tangled web we weave
When first we practice to deceive.

Key Words and Phrases: involvement, entanglement, confusion, illusion, traps, pitfalls.

Subsidiary meanings:

Involvement – confuse, complicate, perplex, involve, entangle, embroil, deception, guile, trickery, pretence, insincerity.

Illusion – misrepresentation, deception, distortion, confuse, sleight of hand, not what it seems, pretence, fraud, trickery, crafty, cunning, hoax, doublecross, take advantage of, pull the wool over one's eyes.

Traps/Pitfalls – lay a trap, entangle, net, trip up, catch out, lure, decoy, entice, tempt, waylay, lie in wait, source of danger, boobytrap, trapdoor, thin ice, powder-keg, trouble spot, hornet's nest, hidden hand, snake in the grass.

THE SYMBOLS OF THE WHITE DICE

WHITE DICE – SIX SPOTS – CROSSROADS

'Dirty work at the crossroads' is a well-known saying which conjures up foul play and nefarious activities. This association has probably come about because murderers and suicides (who were excluded from holy rites) were, at one time, buried at crossroads. And in the case of murderers they were sometimes hanged there too. The ancient Teutonic people used such places for holding sacrifices to their gods and by association they came to be places of execution. During the Middle Ages the crossroads was also used as a rendezvous for witches and demons.

This meeting place of roads is symbolic of a choice of direction, a chance to change direction and just simply what it is – a meeting place.

Key Words and Phrases: hidden surprises, strangers, outsiders that can cause contentions and influence the home and family, decisions.

Subsidiary meanings:
Hidden Surprises – concealed, camouflage, disguise, smokescreen, unintelligible, mask, keep back, reserve, withhold, unexpected, unprepared, sudden, shock, jolt, bolt from the blue, bombshell, revelation, amazing, unguessed, unforseen, not anticipated, unannounced, improbable, not bargained for, without notice.
Strangers/Outsiders – intruder, interloper, foreigner, person in a

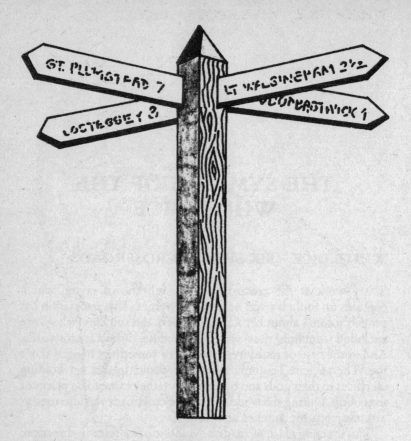

place or in company that he does not belong to, unknown, non-member of the circle or party.

Cause Contentions – create, produce, bring about, result in, breed, stir up, construct, build, form, – quarrels, disputes, clashes, conflicts, trouble, arguments, make mischief, divide, set against, areas of disagreement, jealousy, disharmony, set at odds, clashes.

Influence – jaundice, prejudice, leverage, hold, grip, pressure, cause, pull strings, dominate, work upon, induce, persuade, convince, colour, infect, have a hold on.

Decisions – reach a stage, turning point, moment, opportunity, focus, centre, reach opinion, decree, estimate, calculate, sum up.

WHITE DICE – FIVE SPOTS – CAT

Cats – sleek, cruel and stealthy – are symbols of mystery and occult powers. No self-respecting witch in the Middle Ages would have been without her feline familiar, and many an innocent villager was put to death on the suspicion of witchcraft just for owning one. In classical legend one of the priestesses of Hecate, the queen of witchcraft and sorcery, would often take on the form of a cat. To the Romans the cat was a symbol of liberty and freedom, probably because of the animal's hatred of restraint.

The colour of a cat is often very important as far as superstition and folklore are concerned. However, in America a cat, regardless of colour, seen washing its ears excessively was regarded as a flood warning. Black cats have long been associated with witchcraft and the devil but during the trial of the Chelmsford witches in 1566 a white-spotted cat named Sathan was accused of many nefarious deeds including murder. Black cats are sometimes thought of as lucky although the Chinese dislike them as they are, to them, a warning of sickness. On the island of Guernsey a stranger is expected if a black cat passes the window, and a cat with double claws is doubly lucky and should be treated with great care.

Conway in his book *Demonology and Devil Lore* states that a tri-coloured cat will protect the house in which it lives against fire. He goes on to say that a black cat protects gardens and can cure epilepsy although he doesn't say how.

Key Words and Phrases: home, marriage, the family circle, children, relatives.

Subsidiary meanings:

Home – abode, place of habitation, address, residence, domicile, hang-out, roof over one's head, lair, den, homestead, birthplace, home ground, manor, bricks and mortar, avenue, roost.

Marriage – wedlock, conjugal bliss, matrimony, wedding, nuptials, man and wife, mate, partner, husband, wife, lord and master, other half, pair, joined, couple, for better or worse.

Family Circle – relations, kindred, kith and kin, descendants, ancestors, offspring, flesh and blood, twin, brother, sister, cousin, aunt, uncle, stock, breed, strain, line, tribe, clan.

WHITE DICE – FOUR SPOTS – KNIFE

Come, thick night,
And pall thee in the dunnest smoke of hell
That my keen knife see not the wound it makes
Nor heaven peep through the blanket of the dark
To cry 'Hold, hold!'

Macbeth – Shakespeare.

Knives are not generally looked upon as lucky objects and are usually thought of as the tools of assassins. Because they are sharp

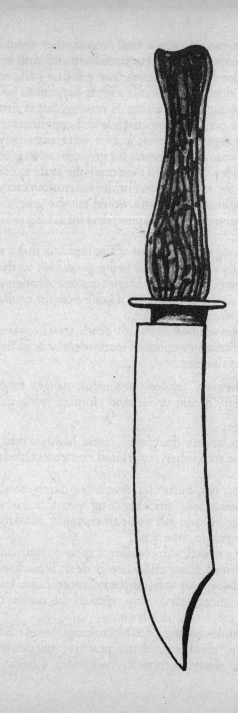

and can inflict a severe cut, or even a fatal wound, they should never be given as presents. They can cut friendship and must be bought, even if the price paid is nominal. The gift of a knife at Easter is thought to be doubly unlucky. If a knife happens to fall on the floor it is a sure sign that a visitor is coming, but if two knives should cross, be prepared for quarrels and arguments.

During the Middle Ages, however, knives were extremely acceptable presents. It was quite common for groomsmen to give them as a present to brides. She would then carry the knife at her wedding ceremony, in the same way that brides today often carry bouquets. In was thought that the knife would cut the groom's love if it was not true but would remain powerless for as long as he gave his devotion.

An old wive's tale along the East Coast of England says that if a knife is found in a baby's cradle it will bring good luck to the infant. This probably stems from an old Danish custom of hanging a bag containing rosemary, salt, bread and a knife over the cradle to welcome the baby when it was born.

Knives have long been symbols of bloody death, treachery and violence. They are a Christian symbol of martyrdom and, to the Buddhists, a stabber of demons.

Key Words and Phrases: tension, argument, danger from over-hastiness, treachery, deceit, underhand plotting, intrigues.

Subsidiary meanings:

Tension – worry, strain, unrest, discontent, stress, highly strung, forces pulling against each other, suppressed excitement likely to burst out.

Argument – disharmony, rift, bickering, friction, quarrels, feud, vendetta, clash, altercation, tiff, breaking point, area of disagreement, at loggerheads, fall out, part company, look for trouble, provoke, wrangle, row with.

Danger from over-hastiness – peril, vulnerability, expose oneself, run the risk, hang by a thread, come under fire, bode ill, hazardous, perilous, chancy, dicey, not safe, slippery, more haste less speed, unprepared, unorganized, snap, spur of the moment, undue urgency, in too much of a hurry.

Treachery/Deceit – double-dealing, doublecrossing, two-faced, dirty trick, perfidy, chicanery, sharp practice, unfaithful, traitorous, disloyal, shady, dishonest, deception, duplicity,

fraud, tricks, lies, not what it seems, untrue, deceptive, play false, make an ass of, let down, leave in the lurch, catch out.
Underhand Plotting/Intrigues – stealthy, dishonest, misleading, crooked, bent, crafty, foxy, scheming, intriguing, not born yesterday, too clever by half, tricky, pull a fast one.

WHITE DICE – THREE SPOTS – HEART

Thou Lord hast made us for Thyself; therefore our hearts are restless until they rest in Thee.

—*St Augustine*

The heart, when employed as an emblem, signifies the centre of illumination and happiness. For this reason it is often portrayed surmounted by flames, a cross, a fleur-de-lis or a crown. Luckenbooths were special tokens (brooches, rings and so on) which were made during the seventeenth and eighteenth centuries in lock-up shops or booths in Edinburgh, hence the name. They were usually fashioned in silver and exchanged between sweet-hearts. They bore a heart-shaped emblem and sometimes two joined hearts surmounted by a crown.

Chambers, in his *Book of Days*, tells of another type of Celtic ring linked with the heart. Claddagh Rings come from the community of fisher folk living in Galway. They seldom inter-marry and cling firmly to many old customs and beliefs. Their curious wedding rings bear the device of two clasped hands holding a heart. These rings have become heirlooms and are passed from mother to eldest daughter. The mother, apparently, ceases to wear a ring when her eldest daughter marries.

The Egyptians believed that the heart was the seat of the soul. It was the only part of the viscera left in the mummy since it was thought of as the centre, indispensible to the body in eternity. On the Day of Judgement they believed that the heart would be weighed and, if it passed the test, its owner would enjoy everlasting life and blessings. A cross resting on a heart was their symbol of goodness. The Egyptians also wore heart-shaped amulets as a protection against sorcerers who could charm the soul from the body. In Far Eastern philosophy the heart, together with the lotus flower and the rose, was viewed as symbolic of the hidden centre – 'hidden' because it is only imagined to exist. It denotes the state achieved through the elimination of separation.

When the body is viewed as a vertical scheme there are three focal points – the sexual organs, the heart and the brain. Because the heart is the central point it takes on the meanings of the other two.

Key Words and Phrases: love, affection, friendship, fondness, passion, desire.

Subsidiary meanings:
Love – desire, gives pleasure, want, need, passion, hunger for, fondness, infatuation, partiality, fascination, affinity, sexual desire, lust, attraction, unable to resist, true love, real thing, possessiveness, jealousy, fondness, liking, fancy, amorous, tender, attractive, charming, flirtation, amour, courtship, sweetheart, boyfriend, suitor, old flame, hold dear.
Friendship – amity, compatibility, fellowship, familiarity, intimacy, kindness, warmth, pal, mate, comrade, amicable, loyal, faithful, staunch, trustworthy, compatible, inseparable, thick as thieves, get pally, get acquainted.

WHITE DICE – TWO SPOTS – STORK

> Constancy is like unto the stork, who wheresoever she fly cometh into no nest but her own.
>
> — *Euphues – Lyly – 1580*

The stork has been viewed by all cultures as a bird of good omen. Storks build freely on the roofs of houses and outbuildings in Europe and, because they are regarded as lucky, they are not discouraged. In the Netherlands it is believed that no house will burn down while there are storks nesting on its roof, while the Chinese say that a house which harbours storks will not be robbed. Northern European children are told that the storks bring babies and drop them down the chimney. This is similar to the gooseberry bush story. Both the gooseberry and the stork are sacred to Venus, so a link in the stories can be found.

Storks are known to be excellent scavengers, besides waging war on all types of vermin. In the Middle Ages, when sanitation was almost unknown, storks were encouraged for the vital service they afforded to mankind. In China it was thought to be a bird which carried on the aims of forefathers and the Hebrews looked on it as a symbol of gratefulness, kindness, mercy and piety.

The stork is an aquatic bird – a fisher – and, because of its feeding habits, is associated symbolically with the waters of creation. It is known as the bringer of children which are found in embryo by the fishing storks in the creative waters of Mother Earth. The only derogatory belief attached to the stork is to be found in Chaucer's time when it was regarded as a symbol of adultery.

The stork received its name, according to a Swedish legend, from flying round the cross of the crucified Jesus crying 'Styrka! Styrka!' (strengthen! strengthen!).

Key Words and Phrases: new beginnings, ideas, projects, fertility, inventiveness, ingenuity.

Subsidiary meanings:
New Beginnings – not previously in existence, modern, recent, unheard of, up to date, revolutionary, move with the times, point at which things begin, source, origin, fresh starts, come into existence, enter on, embark upon, tackle, commence, set the ball rolling, take the plunge.

Ideas – notion, thought, concept, theory, percept, mental image, imagination, fancy, fantasy, brain wave, discovery, wheeze, contrive, reflection, observation.

Projects – plans, schemes, designs, organisation, programmes, proposal, strategy, programme of work, blueprints, plans of attack, approach to problem, schedule, devise.

Fertility – productiveness, booming economy, prosperity, fruitful, abundant, prolific, teeming, inventive, give birth, bring forth.

Inventiveness/Ingenuity – creativeness, all my own work, original, not imitation, uniqueness, independence, one's own, genuine article, first-hand, unimitated, thoughtful, brainwork, association of ideas, wily, foxy, dodge, wrinkle, little game, knowledgeable, canny, too clever for, know a trick or two.

WHITE DICE – ONE SPOT – SUN

> The sun, centre and sire of light,
> The keystone of the world-built arch of heaven.
>
> *Festus: Heaven — P. J. Bailey*

The sun has gathered to itself many legends, beliefs and superstitions. Without the sun there would be no light or life in the world and it became the chief object of worship of many primitive peoples. The Egyptians saw it as Ra's golden boat sailing the sky, the Indians of Central America as the resting place of the dead and the Aborigines believed that it was created from an emu's egg which was tossed into the sky. The Hebrews saw it as symbolic of Jehova's might and it is also a Christian emblem of the Virgin Mary.

In astrology the sun governs the spirit, vitality, rulership, the will to live, organization and power. He is the ruler of the spirit, of the Zodiac sign of Leo, and the first day of the week – Sunday. The sun also has phallic attributes because of its procreative power and is thought of as a masculine force.

Primitive people regarded the sun as a wanderer making his endless journeys across the sky. He was also a life-giver because his arms (his rays) reached down to man and gave him the breath of life. Muspelheim is the name given in Norse mythology to a light and glowing land to the south and it was believed that the sun had

been sprayed from there into the heavens.

The sun is yet another dice symbol with Tarot links and, in this case, direct correspondences. The nineteenth card of the Tarot Trumps is called 'The Sun' and stands for glory, illumination, good health and success.

Key Words and Phrases: ambition, drive, forceful energy, success, power, achievement.

Subsidiary meanings:

Ambition – intention, calculation, purpose, determination, resolve, pursuit, project, design, desire, objective, hell-bent, out for, have in mind, intend for oneself, dream of, aspiration, expectation, vision, wishful, would-be, promise oneself.

Drive/Forceful Energy – vigour, power, force, energy, sparkle, fire, ardour, glow, enthusiasm, passion, powerful, nervous energy, bold, spirited, vivacious, impassioned, decisive.

Success – glory, happy ending, success story, time well spent, accomplishment, completion, triumph, victory, win the game, no defeat, master, effective, efficient, fruitful, profitable, unbeaten, make the grade, come off well, pull it off, bear fruit, crow over, get the better, win hands down, romp home, with flying colours.

Power – potency, control, sway, influence, ability, authority, manage, strength, force, superior, more than a match, compelling, have what it takes, prestige, leadership, government, lay down the law.

Achievement – gain, advance, headway, advancement, promotion, reaching goal, succeeding.

THE SYMBOLS OF THE GREEN DICE

GREEN DICE – SIX SPOTS – FRUIT-TREE

He that would have the fruit must climb the tree.

Gnomologia — Thomas Fuller No.2366

The symbol of the fruit tree has been replaced on modern sets of fortune dice by the pound or dollar sign but its significance remains the same – money, and all that it implies, as a reward for hard work. The fruit tree, as a symbol, was more appropriate in former times when farming communities regarded a good harvest of fruits as the reward for their labours throughout the year.

Different cultures have viewed the fruit tree and the fruit that it bears in various ways. In northern countries the apple figures heavily whilst in more southerly climes the orange, fig and grape vine are regarded as symbols of fruitfulness. In Chinese symbology fruit trees represent not only fertility but also longevity.

The tree itself represents life, growth, proliferation and the centre of the world. And because its roots spread out underground and its branches reach up towards the sky it symbolizes an upward trend. Fruit has been linked with the egg which is the seed of generation, the mystery of life. The apple features in the Adam and Eve story in the Old Testament when the first two people on earth were tempted by the serpent with an apple. It is linked with earthly desires and temptation. Which brings us back to the

modern day pound sign – money, one of the greatest earthly desires.

Key Words and Phrases: money, possessions, property, appearances, things worked for.

Subsidiary meanings:

Money – wealth, riches, luxury, opulence, affluence, solidity, substance, independence, resources, capital, fortune, well-heeled, flush, have the means, be able to pay, make ends meet, feather the nest, funds, cash, currency.

Possessions – ownership, belongings, rightfully owned, personal, one's own property, moveables, goods and chattels, belongings, effects, valuables.

Property – possessions, estate, assets, land, holdings, real estate, birthright, heritage.

Appearances – impressions created, externals, look of things, show, effect, visual impression, ostentation, how things seem, on the face of it, protocol, convention, custom, done thing, correctness, polish, manners.

Things worked for – desires, courses of action, ambition, aspiration, things that appeal, what has been achieved, gathered, earned.

GREEN DICE – FIVE SPOTS – GOBLET

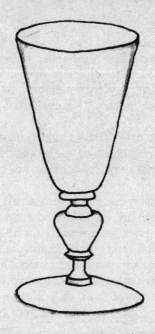

The goblet has the same symbolic meanings as the cup, which are – friendship, good fellowship, intuition, prudence and love. It is a symbol of the human heart. Because of its associations with the Holy Grail, of Arthurian Legend, it also represents a quest or the search for something. Although in their book *The Holy Blood and the Holy Grail* the authors (Michael Baigent, Richard Leigh and Henry Lincoln) assert that the grail was not a goblet but a bloodline.

The goblet, or chalice, has been widely used in religious ceremonies and is one of the main components of the Christian Communion Service. In other doctrines it has been used as a receptacle for the blood of a sacred king or deity. The symbolic links with the heart are carried on into the Tarot deck. 'Chalices' (goblets) was the name given to the heart suit which signified passion.

In Roman mythology it was associated with Mercury, the winged messenger of the gods, when in his role of leading the soul to unknown regions or presiding at birth.

Key Words and Phrases: celebrations, food and wine, entertainment, fun, debauchery, search for the unattainable.

Subsidiary meanings:

Celebrations – ceremonies, functions, occasions, do's, festive occasion, fête, festivity, rejoicing, fireworks, congratulations, toasts, special day, day to remember, field day, great day, anniversary, make much of, kill the fatted calf, do honour to, jubilations.

Food and wine – eat, drink and be merry, toast, pledge, drink to, raise glasses to, drink health of, eating and drinking, banqueting, wining and dining, orgy, feast, blow out, spread, good living, gourmet, epicure.

Entertainment – amusement, pleasure, interest, delight, diversion, relaxation, merriment, leisure, good time, round of pleasure.

Fun/Debauchery – sport, amusement, social gatherings, parties, feasts, revels, high jinks, spree, night out, frolic, prank.

Search for the unattainable – seek information, hunt, seek, look for, something whose presence is expected, investigate, quest, impossible, not to be had, hopeless, no chance, elusive, unavailable, too hard, unachievable, not feasible.

GREEN DICE – FOUR SPOTS – KEY

Mystery or enigma, the means to perform a task, threshold of the unconscious, access to knowledge – the key is symbolic of all these things. And to find a key signified the beginning of a difficult quest before the actual discovery of the treasure.

The key, as a symbol, is possibly even older than the Swastika which is regarded as being one of the earliest symbols employed by man. To the ancient Greeks and Romans the single key was an important mascot – it represented the Key of Life. These talismanic keys were made of silver, which was the metal of Diana. She, under her alias Jana, presided over the Threshold, although

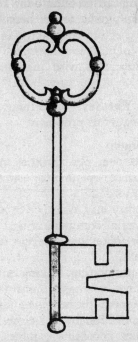

she was also joint custodian of the Doorway with her male counterpart Janus. She was also the guardian of child-bearing women and in this role kept watch over the Threshold of Life.

These talismanic keys were also closely connected with the Key of the Door through which the prayers of the devout reached the gods. They were a symbol of the entrance to Life and were worn to promote 'Remembrance of things past and foresight for things to come.' Sometimes their handles were heart-shaped and they became symbolic of guarded affection. They were given as love tokens – to lock or unlock the door of the heart.

The Greeks often wore the silver keys of Hecate attached to rings. This is another form of the Key of the Door symbolism. Hecate was the goddess of magical rites and of the underworld. She had power over the spirits of the dead and the key formed a link between the living and those departed. There is also a morphological connection between the Egyptian Nem Ankh sign – the anserated cross – the key of eternal life, which opens up the gates of death on to immortality.

The Romanies believed that if a door key was hung upside-down near their beds it would protect them from harm and ensure peaceful sleep. A ring of any kind, in this instance the ring at the top of the key, was a charm against Mare, the spirit of the night and bringer of bad dreams. The word 'nightmare' comes from this source.

Key Words and Phrases: opportunity, doors opening or closing, chances, answers to problems.

Subsidiary meanings:

Opportunity – chance, openings, facilities, free hand, favourable juncture, good chance, opening for action, to do, find, make, get, seize, give, afford.

Doors – threshold, entry into, entrance or exit, means of access, approach to, means of communicating.

Opening – chance for action, gap, passage, introduction, preface, beginning, entrance.

Closing – excluding, prohibiting, locking-out, preventing, disbar, shutting out, exiling, barring, terminating, ending, finishing, chance lost, completion, finished, over, no second chance, time up, come to an end, brought to a close, once and for all.

Chances – opportunities, possibility, gambles, risks, by chance, just happen, way things fall out, fortune, undesigned occurrences, fate.

Answers to problems – solutions, keys, clues, ways to solve, light, illumination, clarification, the secret, how to handle, what to do in the circumstances, – difficulties, worries, make one despair, complications, questions, something in need of solution, difficult to solve.

GREEN DICE – THREE SPOTS – LADDER

> Alas! we make
> A ladder of our thoughts, where angels step,
> But sleep ourself at the foot: our high resolves
> Look down upon our slumbering acts.
>
> — *Landon*

The ladder is a very ancient symbol which represents ascension or the communication between different levels. Well into Victorian times, heaven was believed to be an actual country and the

Egyptians, particularly, thought that a ladder was necessary to reach this higher level of existence. Many Egyptian tombs have contained ladder-shaped amulets and one line from their *Book of the Dead* runs:

My steps are now in position so that I may see the Gods.

These amulets were worn to supplicate the aid of Horus, the god of ladders, to leave behind all earthly things and to reach the greater heights. Some paintings discovered in the pyramids depicted two ladders. The first for the soul to climb out of the darkness of the grave and the second for the soul to ascend to the everlasting light.

The ladder features prominently in many religious teachings, and in Christianity it is seen as Jacob's Ladder with its seventy-two rungs reaching up into the clouds. Bettinis' *Libro del monte santo di Dio* (Florence 1477) depicts steps superimposed on a mountain. Each of the eleven rungs are named after a virtue – humility, prudence, temperance, fortitude, justice, awe, mercy, science, counsel, understanding and finally, wisdom.

The superstitious belief which still holds strong to this day, that it is unlucky to walk under a ladder, has its roots in the distant past. It is necessary to make a detour around the ladder to avoid disturbing, or indeed incurring the wrath of, any spirits who may be using it on their ascent to heaven. This superstition is reinforced by another piece of symbolism – a ladder when leant against a wall forms a triangle (the ladder, the wall and the ground) which was a symbol of life in olden times. Therefore it was thought extremely dangerous to walk beneath and break the imaginary triangle.

Key Words and Phrases: ambition, enthusiasm, new projects, ways up or down, up to you how you play things.

Subsidiary meanings:

Ambition – intention, calculation, purpose, determination, resolve, pursuit, project, design, desire, objective, hell-bent, out for, have in mind, intend for oneself, dream of, aspiration, expectation, vision, wishful, would-be, promise oneself.

Enthusiasm – ardent zeal, forceful energy, drive, vigour, power, force, sparkle, fire, ardour, glow, passion, nervous energy, spirited, vivacious, impassioned, decisive.

New Projects – not previously in existence, modern, recent, unheard of, up-to-date, revolutionary, move with the times, plans, conceptions, intentions, calculations, designs, schemes, proposals, objects, things to be done, strive after, aim at.

Ways up or down – courses, routes, methods, roads to take, means, potentials for, facilities, provide the route, course to a higher place, position, degree, amount, value, in an ascending direction/towards or to a lower or inferior place, level, position, state.

Up to you – your choice, what you make of it, nobody else can do things for you, you hold the controls.

GREEN DICE – TWO SPOTS – LIGHTNING

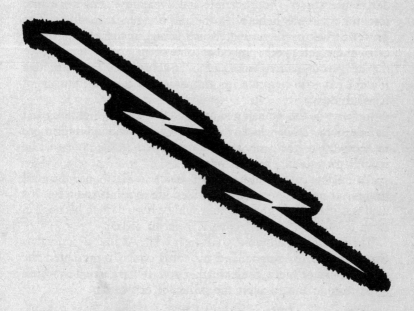

It is too rash, too unadvised, too sudden;
Too like the lightning, which does cease to be
'Ere one can say 'It lightens'.

Romeo and Juliet (Act II Sc 2) — *Shakespeare*

Lightning was, and still is, an awesome and frightening sight. It struck terror into the hearts of primitive man and many superstitions and beliefs have grown up around it. The Buddhists believed that the lightning god flashed in order to lighten the sky and enable the thunder god to take accurate aim to kill the wicked.

The Chinese revered it and regarded it as the dragon's tongue or the fire of heaven, and in Shivaism its flash was related to the glance from the third eye of Shiva, the destroyer of all material forms. This 'flash' has also been related to dawn and to illumination. The everyday sayings, 'It came to me in a flash' and, 'a sudden flash of inspiration', illustrate this aspect of lightning – that of inspiration and a glimpse of truth.

From a negative viewpoint lightning represents danger, destructive force – both terrible and dynamic – vengeance and, sometimes, it was believed to be the bringer of madness. The Tower Struck by Lightning, which is one of the Major Arcana cards in the Tarot pack, embodies some of these ideas. It alludes to the dangerous consequences of over-confidence (a destructive force) or the sin of pride, meglomania and the wild pursuit of fanciful ideas.

Jupiter was the Roman god associated with both lightning and thunderbolts. Oaks, which were believed to attract lightning more than any other tree, were consecrated to him in the hope that he would spare them from his wrath.

An ancient superstitious belief was that Earth had magical restorative powers because it provided life to plants and trees. If a man was struck by lightning he would be buried up to his neck in earth to ensure a rapid recovery from his ordeal.

The Hindus often wore a talisman which is best described as two arrow heads surrounded by cords which represented the thunderbolts of Indra, their weather god. It was carried to secure good fortune and to avert the influence of demons.

Key Words and Phrases: speed, hurry, quick actions, thoughtlessness, unexpected anger directed against you, wrong end of the stick.

Subsidiary meanings:

Speed – swiftness, quickness, greased lightning, move fast, tear, rush, flat out, in double time.

Hurry – move fast, bowl along, in double quick time, rush, no time to lose, break-neck speed, unable to wait, work against time, scurry, bustle, don't waste a minute, brook no delay.

Thoughtlessness – unthinking, inattentive, unwise, unreflective, mindless, not thinking, inconsiderate, careless, unseeing, rash, without consideration, foolish, miscalculated.

Unexpected Anger – surprise, shock, amazing, unguessed, unforseen, not anticipated, not bargained for, taken aback . . . resentment, displeasure, ill-humour, indignation, wrath, irritation, exasperation, hot displeasure, crossness, not amused, fury, burst of indignation, short temper.

Wrong end of the stick – misunderstanding, misinterpret, get wrong, blunder, not properly explained, not in the picture.

GREEN DICE – ONE SPOT – SNAIL

Like snails I see the people go
Along the pavement, row on row;
And each one on his shoulder bears
His coiling shell of petty cares –
The spiral of his own affairs.

From a Street Corner — Eleanor Hammond

The humble snail immediately conjures up a picture of a slow and clumsy creature dragging itself along the ground carrying its 'home' on its shoulders. To many it is a repulsive sight but mankind can learn an important lesson from the snail and his leisurely pace. In this high-speed world of the twentieth century leisure is an important commodity and certainly something which a snail has plenty of.

Snails have also been linked with concealment because of their ability to hide away in their shells when danger threatens. Taking this one step further – they have somewhere private to go where they are totally alone and can take stock of a situation before they re-emerge. Yet another lesson which we can benefit from – everyone needs somewhere to think, meditate and examine their problems quietly where they will not be disturbed.

Wherever a snail chooses to go he leaves a trail of slime behind him, he leaves his mark and will be remembered. The Celts called this trail the Light of the Lug. Lug was a Celtic deity of light, sky and the sun and Lug's Chain was the Celtic name for the Milky Way or track of souls. They drew parallels between this and the snail's earthly tracks.

Key Words and Phrases: health, slow up, care, think, on guard, no hurried decisions.

Subsidiary meanings:

Health – soundness of body and mind, good constitution, health and strength, fitness, condition, well-being, look after one's self.

Slow up – decelerate, reduce speed, ease up, take things easier, don't rush so much, rein in, moderate, take more time over things.

Care – attention to detail, keep an eye on, be vigilant, more meticulous, alert, on your toes, weather eye open, take care, watch what you're doing, look before you leap.

Think – use your brain, collect your thoughts, cogitate, meditate, contemplate, study, take stock, mull over, digest, examine, concentrate, ruminate, check things over first.

On Guard – vigilant, look out, surveilance, watchful, ready, prepared, attentive.

No hurried decisions – with undue haste, without reflection, on the spur of the moment, without thinking, settlements, conclusions, settle upon a course of action, plan of campaign.

8
HOW TO CAST

Three ordinary dice, each of a different colour, and a flat surface is all that you need for divining with dice. The three colours means that you can identify individual dice and, therefore, relate three lots of common numbers – the dots – to eighteen different symbols. The colours of the dice and the symbol linked with each face, are set out below:

First Dice – RED (which represents the hundreds)
Six	–	Bat
Five	–	Beetle
Four	–	Horseshoe
Three	–	Boat
Two	–	Skull
One	–	Web

Second Dice – WHITE (which represents the tens)
Six	–	Crossroads
Five	–	Cat
Four	–	Knife
Three	–	Heart
Two	–	Stork
One	–	Sun

Third Dice – GREEN (which represents the units)

Six	–	Fruit tree
Five	–	Goblet
Four	–	Key
Three	–	Ladder
Two	–	Lightning
One	–	Snail

You do not have to stay with this particular colour scheme (red/white/green) for your set of dice. But it is important that, once you have chosen your colours, you always interpret them in the same sequence.

Cast your three dice onto a flat surface and note the numbers of the dots on the uppermost faces. Repeat this twice more, noting the dots each time. At this stage, if you only want a quick and, therefore, very general interpretation to your casts, check the individual meanings in the final pages of this book.

The first dice throw will tell you about your (or your querent's) general situation. The second deals with financial and business matters and the third looks at love and affection. For more detailed readings you will also need to study the chapter on symbols and apply some of your own intuitive interpretations to the results.

There is another way to interpret these three casts but first you must decide whether you want a general reading, one with a financial slant or a reading concerning the affairs of the heart. Here you again cast the dice three times and note the numbers. But the first cast covers a period of three months hence, the second six months and the third a year. Look up each number in turn in the interpretations under the heading you have chosen and for more detail study the symbols and their meanings to add 'more meat to the bone'.

Your dice can also be used for short-term divination – the next seven days in fact – simply by totalling the number of spots and ignoring references to symbolic meanings. This is a very elementary method of divination by dice and the results achieved are basic and uncomplicated.

Cast the dice into a circle about seven inches in diameter drawn on a piece of paper. Should any dice roll out of the circle, or fall to the ground, they should be interpreted as follows:

One dice outside the circle – some difficulties, an upset of plans.
Two dice outside the circle – quarrels and arguments.
Three dice outside the circle – good fortune, a wish granted.
Dice which fall on the floor – annoyance and worry in the near
  future.

The spots on the uppermost faces of dice which have landed in the circle should be added up. If the total is less than three the dice have nothing to say. For a total of three or more spots the following interpretations apply:

Three – unexpected and surprising developments should occur almost immediately.

Four – unpleasantness and probably quarrels, discord and discontent.

Five – a wish will be granted, good news from a stranger or help from an unexpected quarter.

Six – discouragement, monetary loss or loss generally.

Seven – problems, difficulties to be overcome, business delays.

Eight – a thoughtless action can lead to trouble, reproach, criticism.

Nine – an engagement or marriage affecting the subject. Reconciliation.

Ten – female – a birth connected with the subject.
          male – a promotion, or some new approach to a problem
                  will be revealed.

Eleven – a loved one will make a journey, partings.

Twelve – an important letter – possibly containing good news, a message bringing the solution to a problem or relief of mind.

Thirteen – temporary unhappiness, sorrow if you continue with some matter in hand.

Fourteen – a friend will help you overcome a problem.

Fifteen – caution both in words and deeds to avoid trouble and problems.

Sixteen – a journey both pleasant and profitable terminating in happiness.

Seventeen – a change of mind, benefit from some matter to be concluded shortly.

Eighteen – success, rewards, happiness and almost immediate good fortune.

To gain further insight the circle can be divided into twelve equal segments radiating out from the centre, each of which should be labelled as follows:

1. The Home
2. Health
3. Wealth
4. Love/Happiness
5. Travel
6. Career
7. Legal Matters
8. Friends
9. Enemies
10. Hopes/Fears
11. The Present
12. The Future

Again three dice are cast into the circle and you should note any which fall outside. This time their numbers and meanings refer to the sections in which they land. The spots on each dice are interpreted as follows:

1. Favourable indications
2. Success depends on maintaining friendly relations
3. Triumph

4. Disappointment
5. Good news
6. Doubt

The spots from the three dice are then totalled for a general reading, as outlined.

9
INTERPRETATIONS

666 – BAT CROSSROADS FRUIT-TREE

General Situation: Annoyances and problems which have been dogging you lately have now run their course. A sudden, unepected jolt will help you to reach an important decision concerning a course of action which is open to you.

Finance/Business: Business matters have definitely been under a cloud recently but a turning point has now been reached and the opportunity to expand will be given to you by someone from outside your usual circle of acquaintances.

Love/Affection: There may have been some arguments between you and your partner which could well have been caused by new acquaintances. You must not air your differences in public – these disagreements will be solved in time.

665 – BAT CROSSROADS GOBLET

General Situation: Be on your guard concerning new friends you may meet at parties or other celebrations – they might have a few tricks up their sleeves which could catch you unawares.

Finance/Business: At work you could afford to relax a little as current, annoying problems will soon be ironed out. Prosperity is just around the corner bringing with it an opportunity to achieve something you have always wanted.

Love/Affection: Try not to make a fool of yourself over someone new you might meet. Forewarned is forearmed.

664 – BAT CROSSROADS KEY

General Situation: Don't allow other people to influence an important decision you will soon have to make. It could be very much to your advantage, but someone who is feeling envious might try to give you dubious advice. You know how to handle the situation. Remember an opportunity like this will not be repeated.

Finance/Business: Opportunity knocks – but will it be to your advantage or will it be more trouble than it's worth? Before you commit yourself financially make sure that there are no hidden surprises. But don't take too long or you may miss your chance.

Love/Affection: If things between you and your partner have been a little stormy lately don't despair, it will pass. Circumstances are about to change and a new and better understanding will develop between you.

663 – BAT CROSSROADS LADDER

General Situation: The opportunity you have been waiting for to pursue a personal ambition is just around the corner and will be revealed to you soon. It could prove to be a turning point in your life and the onus is on you to make the most of this chance. Use your ideas and energy towards a positive end and don't be afraid to be inventive and revolutionary in your ideas.

Finance/Business: The sun is beginning to shine again on your business dealings bringing with it a few surprises which you are not prepared for. A decision will have to be taken which could see you a few rungs higher up the ladder of success.

Love/Affection: You are mistaken if you think that a friendship you are cultivating could bring with it any financial reward. Try not to mix business with pleasure, this is not a good idea.

662 – BAT CROSSROADS LIGHTNING

General Situation: Look before you leap! Don't go making any important decisions without prior consultation with your family or you may find misunderstandings will arise and tempers will become frayed. Put all your cards on the table, think things out very carefully and keep everyone in the picture.

Finance/Business: Where finances are concerned – it would be better to do nothing than to enter into any agreement without first making very careful calculations and studying the viability of the scheme. Good communications must be maintained to keep everyone fully informed and good-humoured.

Love/Affection: Say what you mean – your partner isn't a mind-reader. Don't hide your intentions. The only surprise you should spring is a little present bought on impulse.

661 – BAT CROSSROADS SNAIL

General Situation: You may not be feeling all that well or energetic but things will soon improve as long as you don't try to take on more than you can manage. Slow down a little and take more time to relax. Learn to delegate more often.

Finance/Business: Don't come to any hasty decisions over a business matter. Your resources may be very tightly stretched and any extra strain could prove troublesome. Delay matters for a while and wait until your financial situation improves before taking on any more commitments.

Love/Affection: Don't allow jealousy to cloud matters. Let them run their course and avoid any spur-of-the-moment decisions. There is a surprise in store for you which will certainly be an eye-opener.

656 – BAT CAT FRUIT TREE

General Situation: Family matters and finances have definitely been under a considerable strain during the past months. Fortunately, this run of bad luck is coming to an end and things can only get better. Try not to let it get you down too much.

Finance/Business: Your best plan of action, at present, is to just carry on with the day-to-day administration of your business life and avoid trying anything new or different until financial conditions show some marked improvement.

Love/Affection: Your relationship with your partner seems to have been overshadowed by business worries and problems which you have probably taken home with you. This is only a passing phase. Have you tried sharing your troubles instead of bottling them up?

655 – BAT CAT GOBLET

General Situation: It's just a matter of time before those dark days will be gone for good and you and your family will have cause for celebration. Make the most of life and find time to relax and enjoy yourselves. How about a family holiday somewhere exotic?

Finance/Business: At last things seem to be getting back on to an even keel again and your bank balance is more often black than red. Why not celebrate a little and have a night out with your workmates?

Love/Affection: A family wedding or anniversary celebration is indicated and a passing stroke of good luck will provide the icing on the cake. Get together and have fun.

654 – BAT CAT KEY

General Situation: A windfall will provide you and your family with just the opportunity you have all been waiting for. Make the most of this chance as it could help you out of what has been a worrying situation.

Finance/Business: Financial worries will be a thing of the past if you seize a chance that will soon be offered to you. It will provide the way into a whole new field of operation and also chances and introductions hitherto denied to you.

Love/Affection: A chance meeting for single people could lead to a whole lot more than bargained for. Be ready to seize opportunities and let your feelings be known.

653 – BAT CAT LADDER

General Situation: Troubles appear to be behind you now and the future seems promising. You will have lots of new opportunities, plans and ideas and the energy and will to tackle them. Life will be what you make of it.

Finance/Business: Events behind the scenes have altered circumstances and the chance of promotion is there if you want to take it. A new venture will provide just the opportunity you have been waiting for – something which no one else has the expertise to handle but you.

Love/Affection: You and your partner will now be able to do something which you have always dreamed of together. This new scheme will bring you closer together and will be very rewarding.

652 – BAT CAT LIGHTNING

General Situation: If you are wondering why your family seem to be irritated with you lately it is because they have misunderstood something which you have done. Take the time to explain and don't be in such a hurry in future.

Finance/Business: A business venture involving your family will need careful handling if quarrels and rows are to be avoided. Don't try to do things too quickly and make sure that everyone knows what is expected of them. Preliminary teething troubles will soon be ironed out.

Love/Affection: Don't go flying off the handle at your partner until you are sure you know what you're talking about. You may not be aware of all the facts and could appear a little foolish if you react too quickly.

651 – BAT CAT SNAIL

General Situation: A bad period you are going through which will pass soon, but it is putting extra pressure on your family. You must slow up and take more time to relax.

Finance/Business: This is definitely not the right time to make any important decisions. There are other worries and problems you will need to deal with first. Wait until you have time to discuss matters with your family and don't take on any extra responsibilities for the moment.

Love/Affection: Try to find a little more time to devote to your partner who may be feeling neglected. Don't let your feelings be suppressed because of other things on your mind. Try to be more demonstrative.

646 – BAT KNIFE FRUIT-TREE

General Situation: This could be an unpleasant time for you. Your home and possessions might seem threatened and the strain and tension you are under could be quite considerable. Certain friends are not to be trusted and any hasty actions on your part would only exacerbate the situation. One word of consolation, this is only a temporary state of affairs and in due course things will get back on to a more steady footing again.

Finance/Business: Do nothing, decide nothing, trust no one. It is likely you are surrounded by extremely bad circumstances which threaten your financial position. Try to keep a cool head and ride out of the storm – it will abate eventually.

Love/Affection: Keep an eye on the amount of money your partner is spending and you will save yourself a lot of unpleasantness. Maybe find out what it is that they want to buy so badly and buy it for them.

645 – BAT KNIFE GOBLET

General Situation: Don't allow others to trick you into doing something you really don't want to do. They are not such good friends at all, but are only trying to make you appear stupid. It could be something simple like someone doctoring your drink at a party.

Finance/Business: Don't be too eager to get involved in other peoples' financial schemes even though they may have wined and dined you royally and you feel under an obligation to go along with their plans.

Love/Affection: A quiet candlelit meal for two would be a good way of forgetting an argument and will give you the chance to talk things over with your partner on neutral ground.

644 – BAT KNIFE KEY

General Situation: You might have been feeling uncertain of yourself recently but this will pass. Be careful how you handle matters and under no circumstances act without careful thought.

Finance/Business: This is not the right time for any kind of speculative enterprise but don't just sit there idling away your time. Use this period to calculate your next move.

Love/Affection: You will have the opportunity to meet new people and make new friends but be a little on your guard as a new relationship which may spring up could cause friction and quarrels. It will not be long term.

643 – BAT KNIFE LADDER

General Situation: Something which you have been planning to do for some time is in danger of being sabotaged, not only by your own over-hastiness, but also by someone else who will let you down at the last moment. Avoid possible disappointment by thinking things over and make sure that you are fully in control.

Finance/Business: As fast as you seem to achieve something financially, problems crop up which put you back to square one. In the meantime don't let it get you down and don't try to run before you can walk.

Love/Affection: Your current relationship is going well but don't try to push matters or you could provoke an argument. Tread very carefully if you wish to succeed.

642 – BAT KNIFE LIGHTNING

General Situation: Your best plan of action would be to stay at home with a good book. It seems everything you do goes wrong. It could be your own fault or others working against you. Keep a low profile.

Finance/Business: Be prepared to act quickly. A deal clinched now will be advantageous although colleagues may be taken aback by this fast move and fail to understand your motives.

Love/Affection: Your love life seems confused to say the least at present. Try to be a little more considerate or you could find yourself facing an ill-humoured partner.

641 – BAT KNIFE SNAIL

General Situation: Now is the time to take a break, slow the pace and spoil yourself a little. Give your body a chance to recover after all the strain you've been under lately. Collect your thoughts. By mulling things over you will be able to get a clearer picture of the future.

Finance/Business: Pressure of work seems to be getting you down and just when you need the support and loyalty of colleagues they are too busy with their own schemes and let you down. These problems will not undermine your health if you take your time and get yourself organized.

Love/Affection: Don't let family feuding and quarrels come between you and your partner. Their bickering could well force some decisions upon you that you are not prepared for. Be honest with each other and if it's snap decisions they want, they'll just have to wait while you consider things.

636 – BAT HEART FRUIT-TREE

General Situation: The impression you create to others seems to be very important to you. Try to play down your desire to impress, as your real friends like you for who you are and not what you have.

Finance/Business: An office romance is not really a very good idea, beside distracting you from your work it could cause all sorts of other problems too. You have worked hard for the position you now hold so don't throw it all away because of a moment of weakness.

Love/Affection: Your partner has suddenly decided to 'keep up with the Jones's' – to your cost. Avoid spending too much money on appearances.

635 – BAT HEART GOBLET

General Situation: Good times are coming and the austere conditions you have been living under will give way to one long round of pleasure and amusement. So eat, drink and be merry while it lasts.

Finance/Business: While caution has been the watchword in the past, now is the time to splash out a little and prove to others that you're not such a mean old Scrooge as they thought.

Love/Affection: A wonderful time ahead for you and your partner to relax and enjoy some good living together, and some good loving too! Single people need not frown either – parties, high jinks and love.

634 – BAT HEART KEY

General Situation: Old troubles and problems which you feel have been holding you back have run their course and you are entering a phase full of good opportunities and new beginnings in both your private and professional life.

Finance/Business: If your finances have given you cause for despair in the past – take heart, a close friend will provide you with just the opportunity you have been waiting for to capitalize.

Love/Affection: If you have been feeling a little unloved of late that will certainly not be the complaint now. Friends will rally round and take you out of yourself. An existing relationship will get back onto a better footing or a new involvement seems bound for success.

633 – BAT HEART LADDER

General Situation: Friends could help you to achieve an ambition which you have had for some time. However, success is usually that much sweeter if you have achieved it by yourself. You should find that friends won't mind 'passing the reins over' for a while.

Finance/Business: The chance to make a profit will come from a most unexpected quarter. However, if you let this stroke of good luck go to your head you may lose friends.

Love/Affection: Try not to take advantage of your partner's good nature. it won't help you in the long run and will only serve to alienate them.

632 – BAT HEART LIGHTNING

General Situation: Think before you speak or you could find yourself on your own. Unless you choose your words with care, misunderstandings and acrimony will be the result.

Finance/Business: An outstanding debt that really ought to be paid off could soon be settled if you pushed yourself just a little more – maybe even do a bit of overtime.

Love/Affection: A sudden love or infatuation is probable but whatever you do, don't get too involved as it will alienate your family and gain your friend's disapproval.

631 – BAT HEART SNAIL

General Situation: Where's the fire? All this hurry and haste is really not good for you and healthwise it's already beginning to show. If it's really so important to get things done quickly why not enlist the help of family and friends.

Finance/Business: Overwork and poor health go hand in hand unless you slow up. Delegate more so that you are well enough to enjoy the financial benefits you seem almost certain to reap.

Love/Affection: Don't keep trying to hurry your partner or you could find yourself very much on your own. Instead, let them have their own way a little more and things will show a marked improvement and be happier.

626 – BAT STORK FRUIT-TREE

General Situation: The past and its troubles and worries are a closed chapter. The accent is now on the future and what you make of it. Take the plunge and launch that new idea of yours – it should prove to be a great success.

Finance/Business: That get rich quick idea of yours may not be as outlandish as you first thought. Get some capital behind you (either yours or someone else's) and give it a try. Success is assured and the rewards could be great.

Love/Affection: Your partner has been nursing an ambition for quite a while and the only thing holding them back is funds, or rather lack of them. Give them encouragement and a little financial backing – if you can afford it at present.

625 – BAT STORK GOBLET

General Situation: New projects which you are working on seem to be temporarily dogged by bad luck. Teething troubles abound and just when things are taking shape something else seems to go wrong. These are only passing set-backs and success will be achieved by your own inventiveness and ingenuity. What you do will not go unnoticed.

Finance/Business: It would be a good idea to entertain business associates in order to promote new interests and collect new ideas. Your mind is particularly fertile at present and you may need to seek backing for your schemes which could be best discussed over a meal. Past hindrances are definitely going.

Love/Affection: Any feelings of despondency between you and your partner are going and relationships will get on to a much more stable basis. A birth or christening in the family is possible.

624 – BAT STORK KEY

General Situation: Aches, pains and headaches which have been with you for some time will go because you will be too busy to sit and worry about how you are feeling. This is a time to be creative and develop new ideas, to seek new approaches and to decide new plans of attack. Don't waste it.

Finance/Business: So long as you handle things in the right manner financial problems should be relatively easy to solve. New fund-raising opportunities should be taken when they arise.

Love/Affection: For single people this is not a time to make any proposals concerning the future as there are still past problems to be resolved. Those of you with partners should try to confess something which you have been holding back.

623 – BAT STORK LADDER

General Situation: Stop champing at the bit to get started on new projects. Make sure that your ideas really are viable before you put them to the test. Failure would be unthinkable, so think first – act later.

Finance/Business: If you would only let bygones be bygones you would be able to make more headway in your career. The opportunities are there and you certainly don't lack determination or drive, so forget whatever it is that still wrankles and allow yourself to move with the times.

Love/Affection: Your partner could be extremely irritating. Try to ignore it as much as you can, it will pass. Get on with something you are interested in instead.

622 – BAT STORK LIGHTNING

General Situation: You could probably do with some strenuous exercise – it will help get rid of some of those daily frustrations. Muddles and irksome little problems will exasperate you and if only people would say what they mean life would be much easier. Get these irritations sorted out as soon as you can, then put your mind to more creative use.

Finance/Business: Speculate – but move swiftly, there's no time to lose. Buy at once and be assured of a nice profit when you re-sell.

Love/Affection: Perhaps some private worry has made you a little hesitant when it comes to showing your affections. Remember – he who hesitates is lost. Go ahead and do something positive, you'll be surprised what an effect it will have.

621 – BAT STORK SNAIL

General Situation: You should be feeling in fine fettle at the moment but don't go rocking the boat by getting overtired. Your mind seems to be working overtime and you are full of original ideas and thoughts. Remember that you can't do everything at once.

Finance/Business: A new financial venture stands a good chance of success but don't go counting your chickens too early as quite a lot of things could go wrong if you hurry matters. Time will tell.

Love/Affection: Spend more time with your partner instead of rushing about from one social engagement to another. Put your heads together and make a few positive future plans for just the two of you.

616 – BAT SUN FRUIT-TREE

General Situation: Fate is really giving you a helping hand and you don't seem to be able to put a foot wrong. Whatever you touch is bound to succeed. Go ahead and enjoy yourself.

Finance/Business: The Midas touch is yours – go ahead with your money-making plans and schemes, they really can't fail. Promotion and greater responsibility could be offered which will also bring with it financial gain.

Love/Affection: Come down to earth or you will drive your partner mad. It's all very well to be a walking success story but when you've heard the story for about the third time in one evening it can become more than a little irritating.

615 – BAT SUN GOBLET

General Situation: Hold on – you're so busy trying to get on in the world and doing very well at it that you haven't had a night out for a long time. Why not treat yourself to a visit to the cinema, a meal or maybe even a weekend away visiting friends.

Finance/Business: Don't become too over-confident just because things are really booming for you. Even you can put a foot wrong and a social gaff while out dining with the boss and important clients would not go down very well.

Love/Affection: Be satisfied with what you have, if your partner loves and respects you, what more do you want? It's no good spoiling what you have by searching for something which only exists in your mind.

614 – BAT SUN KEY

General Situation: You hold the key to not only your own pleasure but to the pleasure of those dependent upon you. Don't let something in your past spoil your dreams for the future.

Finance/Business: An acceptable way out of a tricky financial problem is at hand. Try to learn from your mistakes and you shouldn't go wrong again. Examination results will be good.

Love/Affection: Kiss and make up. Your future is with your partner and you must learn to handle problems between you. You can't always be right.

613 – BAT SUN LADDER

General Situation: This is a very favourable time to pursue a long held ambition. You are full of energy and determination and as long as you stay in control of the situation your efforts will be rewarded. Don't allow a ghost from your past to mar your success.

Finance/Business: You are more likely to succeed than to fail but this is no reason to be over-confident and take unnecessary risks. Remember that nothing is one hundred per cent certain until it has been achieved.

Love/Affection: This is a particularly special time for lovers and should you be thinking of marriage now is the time to start making plans. If already married how about a second honeymoon?

612 – BAT SUN LIGHTNING

General Situation: Be prepared to act extremely quickly but not inconsiderately if you want to make the most of an opportunity for advancement which will occur soon. Should something be worrying you healthwise don't keep it to yourself but have it checked out. You will save yourself a lot of needless worry.

Finance/Business: This tendency you have to do everything at break-neck speed could mean that you may miss a golden opportunity.

Love/Affection: What have you been up to that's put you in your partner's bad books again? You really must show more consideration and be a little more caring. How about a little surprise present to show that you do stop and think sometimes.

611 – BAT SUN SNAIL

General Situation: If you really bother to collect your thoughts for just a moment and act with just a little more care and wisdom you will see that it is quite possible to overcome something which has been worrying you lately. Look before you leap and think before you act.

Finance/Business: Fortune is smiling on your affairs and seeds you had sown some time ago are now bearing fruit. However, don't try to harvest everything at once or a few of these fruit could get damaged in the process.

Love/Affection: Your partner may be feeling a little tired and under the weather. Use some of your excess energy to help them out until they can get back on their feet again.

566 – BEETLE CROSSROADS FRUIT-TREE

General Situation: A specific ambition which you have been relentlessly pursuing will bring a sudden surprise. A person from outside your direct family circle could spring on you an offer which could bring benefits.

Finance/Business: Hard work is finally going to pay dividends. A sudden chance decision taken over something you have been working on will bring financial rewards which will benefit not only you, but those close to you.

Love/Affection: Go ahead with ideas which may mean some financial outlay. This is a wise thing to do and will be much appreciated by your partner.

565 – BEETLE CROSSROADS GOBLET

General Situation: Don't go turning down social invitations because of your dedication to duty. Everyone needs to allow themselves a little time to relax, see friends and pursue hobbies. Is there someone who can deputize for you for a while?

Finance/Business: It's really been a long, hard struggle to get your latest venture off the ground and only your tireless patience has made it work. Take a breather before you get wrapped up in any new project.

Love/Affection: Why not treat your partner to something a little special – it's rather nice to have a surprise treat occasionally and you could do with a little diversion too. Make it an occasion to be looked back on with pleasure.

564 – BEETLE CROSSROADS KEY

General Situation: All that hard work and study you did when everyone else was out enjoying themselves is about to pay off in a most unexpected way. You will be at a crossroads in your life and you will have to decide on a course of action and stick to it.

Finance/Business: An unexpected windfall could provide you with financial security and put you back on your feet again. Pay off all those worrying outstanding debts and keep a tighter grip on your purse strings in future.

Love/Affection: Don't go feeling unloved and unlovable, affection for you is there but it may not necessarily be shown as you would like. Give it a chance – it'll come out eventually.

563 – BEETLE CROSSROADS LADDER

General Situation: If anyone deserves recognition for sheer hard work, you do. Your salvation will come from a most unexpected quarter but don't let that worry you. Convert your dreams into realities and make the most of a very good offer you are sure to receive soon.

Finance/Business: It's all very well being ambitious but the only way you will climb the ladder of success is by lots of hard work, repeated efforts and resolution. You can do it and the rewards are great.

Love/Affection: The old love life looks in for a stormy time, try to find out if relatives have been interfering again. It's surprising how much trouble can be stirred up by a seemingly harmless remark. A move of house to another area might help.

562 – BEETLE CROSSROADS LIGHTNING

General Situation: Are you really surprised that your family are complaining? Try not to get so involved in a new hobby or other interest that you don't have time for anything or anyone else. Try to be a little less thoughtless and you could be in for a few pleasant surprises.

Finance/Business: A new workmate or colleague could well be the cause of disputes and arguments amongst those you work with. You would be well advised not to get involved or this could make matters worse and even upset your own future plans and ambitions.

Love/Affection: Someone close to you is about to make a revelation you had not bargained for. Make sure that you understand what they want as a misunderstanding over this could result in short tempers and ill-humour all round.

561 – BEETLE CROSSROADS SNAIL

General Situation: A surprise opportunity will need a great deal of thought and a thorough checking out before you reach a decision. If the general everyday pressures of life seem to be weighing a little heavily on you at present, try to keep calm and deal with them one step at a time.

Finance/Business: You could be in for a very pleasant surprise which you certainly had not bargained for. It could be to do with money or property but is more likely to be concerned with a more intimate article such as a piece of jewellery or an item of furniture.

Love/Affection: You really must stop being so romantic and with your head in the clouds where your affections are concerned. Take time to weigh things up and be a little more materialistic in your future approach to personal situations.

556 – BEETLE CAT FRUIT-TREE

General Situation: Try not to feel too despondent and that you will never get all the things you are working so hard for. Talk things over with your family – you may be able to enlist their help or get some new ideas from them. Keep at it, you really can do it.

Finance/Business: As far as income is concerned this is a really good time for you and things are ticking over nicely. Put your efforts into long-term projects rather than trying any get-rich-quick schemes which could prove to be your downfall.

Love/Affection: People around you would seem to be getting more out of life than you. Take a really good look at what you have going for you and you'll be surprised how much you take for granted. Get your values straight.

555 – BEETLE CAT GOBLET

General Situation: You and your family really do have something to celebrate – all that hard work and dedication will now start to pay off.

Finance/Business: Everyone else may have said that your project was doomed from the start but your determination and 'never say die' attitude has proved them all wrong. Resist the temptation to crow about it but by all means enjoy your much deserved success.

Love/Affection: Put a little romance back into your life, perhaps a candlelit supper for two at a nice intimate little restaurant or even a special supper at home with your partner – soft lights and soft music are a must now.

554 – BEETLE CAT KEY

General Situation: Help is at hand, and a problem which you have found difficult to solve will then be seen in a different light. Try to be a little more cheerful as a new phase in your life is coming which will be full of good opportunities.

Finance/Business: Your own financial worries and problems will have to take second place for the time being as someone in your family circle will need your help and advice about a tricky situation they are in. You'll be glad you bothered.

Love/Affection: Don't try quite so hard to impress people and make them like you. Just try being yourself for a change. You'll be surprised what a difference it will make.

553 – BEETLE CAT LADDER

General Situation: This is what you've been waiting so long for – your chance for success. However, you must play your cards very close to your chest as there's always someone who will steal your ideas if they get a chance.

Finance/Business: Money matters are definitely showing an upwards trend at long last. However, it would not be advisable to go buying something frivolous and expensive, at this time.

Love/Affection: You may be faced with making a choice between what your partner wants and your own personal ambition. Allow common-sense to rule the situation.

552 – BEETLE CAT LIGHTNING

General Situation: A niggling little health problem which has been with you for some time will seem to improve overnight. Also now is the time to solve a personal problem provided that you act swiftly but not foolishly.

Finance/Business: This is a lesson that everyone has to learn at some time in their lives – you can't expect to get something you want and give nothing in return. The only way to get what you want is by sheer hard work.

Love/Affection: Emotionally you're in for a very busy time, and if you are happy with how things are going then encourage them, but don't delay too long as indecision from you may be mistaken for indifference.

551 – BEETLE CAT SNAIL

General Situation: Although other people, particularly your family, may seem to be interfering with or hindering your plans, try not to let this annoy you too much. After all, if you actually think over what they have been saying, you might find they have a point.

Finance/Business: Now is a time to formulate new ideas and think about new projects but seek professional advice before you take any definite steps. You may not agree with the advice but don't dismiss it out of hand.

Love/Affection: Be a little more patient as far as your partner is concerned. Other people have feelings too although they may not be the same as yours on every subject. Guard against spur of the moment actions, it's not worth the risk.

546 – BEETLE KNIFE FRUIT-TREE

General Situation: Do you ever get that feeling that someone is being friendly because of what you have rather than who you are? Try to find out who it is and make sure you are not being deceived.

Finance/Business: However persuasive those salesmen are and however foolproof their schemes might seem, don't invest any money unless you have essential guarantees.

Love/Affection: Although your partner may seem a little dull at times, stick with that one however sorely tempted you may be. After all it is better the devil you know than the devil you don't.

545 – BEETLE KNIFE GOBLET

General Situation: Try not to rely too much on others as you could be let down at a time when you most need that extra pair of hands to see you through. Instead, rein in a little and keep matters very much under your own control.

208

Finance/Business: At first glance everything seems to be in order and running well but there is still an underlying feeling that all is not as it should be. Check up on figure work and, if appropriate, do a bit of stocktaking too.

Love/Affection: Don't do anything that might rock the boat. Things are going very nicely between you and your partner and it would be a pity to spoil this mood of good will.

544 – BEETLE KNIFE KEY

General Situation: Your chance is coming to settle old scores with someone who has repeatedly let you down in the past. Something has to be done to clear the air and settle past complaints once and for all.

Finance/Business: Don't be tempted to use others in order to gain your own ends financially. It's not a good idea and one which could quite easily backfire with disastrous results.

Love/Affection: If your partner should somehow upset you try not to over-react and fall out over it. It was not done with the intention to deceive and is better off forgotten.

543 – BEETLE KNIFE LADDER

General Situation: Your unbending desire to reach a personal goal could lead you into dangerous territory. Try not to annoy others and just for once take 'no' for an answer and be satisfied. Make the effort to be more thoughtful for a change.

Finance/Business; How about helping someone else out for a change as you can quite easily afford it at present. You'll be surprised what a rewarding experience it can be!

Love/Affection: Instead of worrying about whether your partner is somehow losing interest in you, it would be a good idea to be a little more demonstrative yourself. You know how you feel but how long is it since you last told them. it could well ease the tension you have both been feeling of late.

542 – BEETLE KNIFE LIGHTNING

General Situation: Avoid arguments if you can at the moment.

What you really ought to do is to slow down and take things a little easier – tiredness and strain from overworking could affect your health in the long term.

Finance/Business: Don't allow a colleague to trick you into doing something on the spur of the moment for which you are not prepared. This will only lead to misunderstandings because you were not properly briefed.

Love/Affection: You ought to pay attention to what your partner has to say or you could find yourself in the wrong. Make every effort to understand what he or she really means.

541 – BEETLE KNIFE SNAIL

General Situation: It would be a good idea to keep complaints to yourself for the time being. Make sure that you really do have a valid grievance before you air it.

Finance/Business; You may find yourself a little behind with payments or instalments of some sort. You must not let this worry you as it will be possible to catch up again although this is something which cannot be done quickly.

Love/Affection: If your partner seems to be feeling a bit cantankerous and quarrelsome; make sure that it's not you who gets the rough edge of their tongue. Keep your head down and wait for the storm to pass.

536 – BEETLE HEART FRUIT-TREE

General Situation: Get out of the rat race for five minutes and spend some time with your family and friends. The indications are that you all need a short holiday.

Finance/Business: Just this once it might not be a bad thing to let your heart be your guide in a business venture instead of going by the book. Use your intuition.

Love/Affection: You and your partner should let your hair down and enjoy yourselves instead of always being conventional. Be a little outrageous – it could be fun!

535 – BEETLE HEART GOBLET

General Situation: Pleasant and happy times are in store for you in the company of your family and close friends. Enjoy life to the full and grab opportunities to celebrate when they present themselves.

Finance/Business: Your advice on a financial matter will be sought by a friend and should not be given grudgingly. You never know when you may need help one day.

Love/Affection: You and your partner will be feeling very much in tune during the coming period. Your relationship will seem to strengthen and become more exciting.

534 – BEETLE HEART KEY

General Situation: Just when you were beginning to despair of ever solving some longstanding problems a friend will point you in the right direction to succeed. From then on it's up to you.

Finance/Business: Have you ever considered going into partnership with a friend? You should, as a chance to do so will arise very soon and the rewards could be considerable provided that you both pull together.

Love/Affection: Someone who you once regarded as being very special is about to come back into your life. This will mean not only new opportunities but a few problems too.

533 – BEETLE HEART LADDER

General Situation: There are things to be done, new plans to be made and fresh targets to aim for. And you have plenty of friends who are only too willing to lend a hand and get you started.

Finance/Business: Financial security is always something which you have aimed at. You will have to make a choice about a new career which could provide just this. Think carefully though, as some schemes could backfire.

Love/Affection: Put a little bit of sparkle back into your private life. You may have been working so hard lately that you didn't notice the fire going out.

532 – BEETLE HEART LIGHTNING

General Situation: Don't just sit about day-dreaming of what might be, get up and do something positive. Once you've taken the plunge you'll be surprised just how much you can achieve in a short space of time.

Finance/Business: Provided that you are prepared to work hard and don't give in when the going gets a little tough, your financial position will improve beyond all recognition.

Love/Affection: You and your partner are in for a busy time when you'll be called upon to make snap decisions. This will have a very positive effect upon your relationship and you will both benefit in one way or another.

531 – BEETLE HEART SNAIL

General Situation: Others seem to be holding you back, especially your family. You will find this particularly irritating but if you take time to think about it they could be right. Ease up a bit, if you carry on overdoing things your health could suffer.

Finance/Business: Financially you really are in limbo at present. You have the drive and determination to succeed but don't seem to be able to find the right direction in which to channel it. Don't make any hurried decisions.

Love/Affection: Have a really good look at your relationship before making any plans for the future. Your partner may not be thinking along the same lines as you and should be given time to think things over. Be patient.

526 – BEETLE STORK FRUIT-TREE

General Situation: Now is the time to branch out and try something new. You've had the idea planned out in your mind for some months and it will only take a little application on your part to set things rolling.

Finance/Business: Promotion or a new role in your working life is indicated. This will be a busy period with new projects to be set up and fresh targets to aim for. An increase in income is likely.

Love/Affection: You really can't buy someone's affections – so don't try. Just be yourself and resist the temptation to turn someone's head with expensive presents.

525 – BEETLE STORK GOBLET

General Situation: Relax and enjoy yourself. Plan ahead for both leisure and work.

Finance/Business: If you're looking for something to invest in – anything to do with the catering trade looks promising. And if you only have a little cash, why not put down a crate or two of wine?

Love/Affection: A wonderful time for lovers whether married or single. Life will be one long round of pleasure with plenty to celebrate and some pleasant discoveries to make.

524 – BEETLE STORK KEY

General Situation: Come on, stir yourself. There's lots to be done and much to be gained. Forget your problems, you must move with the times and try something new for a change.

Finance/Business: If you've had some new ideas lately which could benefit not only you but your employer, make them known as soon as possible. This could be just the opportunity you've been waiting for.

Love/Affection: Harmonious would be the best way to describe your private life these days. Not only are you feeling happy and content but your partner feels the same way too.

523 – BEETLE STORK LADDER

General Situation: Life is what you make of it and your chance to make a dream come true is coming soon. Be ready to act and don't allow minor obstacles to put you off course.

Finance/Business: If you're tired of working for someone else this could be your chance to go it alone, but be prepared to work long hours to get the scheme off the ground.

Love/Affection: How about combining business with pleasure? You and your partner make a good team and neither of you are afraid of hard work. You've both always dreamed of setting up on your own – think about it.

522 – BEETLE STORK LIGHTNING

General Situation: A new idea or scheme which you have decided to pursue is not something which will be quickly achieved. It will require a great deal of thought and determination if this goal is to be achieved. An interesting time ahead.

Finance/Business: A new venture, possibly your own brain-child, is now viable but make sure that you have done your homework properly and haven't tried to cut corners. Don't sign any contracts or enter into any agreements hastily – read the small print with care. A break with tradition, however, could be to your advantage.

Love/Affection: A new romance or friendship seems likely to blossom very quickly, but don't do something foolish which you may regret later. Also don't become so infatuated that you forget all your other friends and interests. Get to know the person better before you make any long-term decisions.

521 – BEETLE STORK SNAIL

General Situation: You really must pay more attention to your health, even a little exercise is better than none at all. A few early nights wouldn't go amiss either if you want to be in peak condition to put all your new plans and ideas into action soon.

Finance/Business: Prosperity for you is just around the corner. Keep your ears and eyes open and be prepared to act. It would be a shame to miss a heaven-sent opportunity because you were caught napping at the crucial moment.

Love/Affection: You and your partner would both benefit from a few quiet nights at home just watching the television, reading a book or just generally relaxing. That candle won't burn at both ends for ever!

516 – BEETLE SUN FRUIT-TREE

General Situation: There really isn't any situation that you couldn't get the better of and come out on top. You will be full of energy and the desire to get things done will be very much in evidence.

Finance/Business: How can you possibly fail? It's almost as if you had the Midas touch as everything you become involved in pays off very handsome dividends. Even the odd silly gamble turns out to be a winner – but don't let it all go to your head.

Love/Affection: You may be feeling on top of a wave but is your partner? Make sure that you share your success and try not to be too full of yourself. A little more humility wouldn't go amiss.

515 – BEETLE SUN GOBLET

General Situation: Make hay while the sun shines and enjoy the fruits of your labours. Your devotion to duty has brought you success and you should share it with family and friends by celebrating a little.

Finance/Business: Don't allow very persuasive sales talk to turn your head. Keep your mind on your own personal goals and look extremely carefully at any offers you may be made that seem too good to be true – there's sure to be a catch somewhere.

Love/Affection: This will be a wonderful, happy time for lovers of all ages. However, don't be tempted to hide yourselves away – get out and about more and above all enjoy yourselves.

514 – BEETLE SUN KEY

General Situation: There will be a number of important opportunities coming your way – but you must look out for them. Talk over your future plans and ambitions with someone whose opinion you value but, above all, be ready to act.

Finance/Business: Opportunity is soon going to knock so make sure that it's you who opens the door to financial advancement. This could be the answer to all your problems. Act now!

Love/Affection: The scene is set for you to have a very happy and loving time provided that you take the initiative and don't hang back. For single people with marriage in mind there couldn't be a better time to pop the question and plan your future together.

513 – BEETLE SUN LADDER

General Situation: However wild and ambitious your ideas may seem, you couldn't ask for a better time to put them to the test. At the moment your life can be what you want to make of it.

Finance/Business: Before you forge ahead with some new scheme which will take all your time, energy and, perhaps, a lot of your hard-earned capital, just make sure that all the preliminary paper work is in order. For instance – are you properly insured?

Love/Affection: There's more to you than meets the eye and your partner will be surprised and delighted with some plans you've been making for you both.

512 – BEETLE SUN LIGHTNING

General Situation: However determined you may be to get a job done as quickly as possible, do be careful! Especially with machinery. Accidents happen so quickly so don't get careless.

Finance/Business: Try not to get too carried away, keep your financial transactions within a limit which you can afford. The temptation to overspend will be very strong. Resist it.

Love/Affection: Try not to upset matters by being selfish and getting so wrapped up in your own thoughts that you don't consider others. This could quite easily cause arguments and displays of temper from your partner.

511 – BEETLE SUN SNAIL

General Situation: Healthwise you will be feeling much fitter and more active than you have done for some time. However, use this new-found vitality carefully or it may not last.

Finance/Business: Your business outlook is first-class and your future prospects also look good. Don't go and spoil things by trying to cut corners or by making thoughtless errors of judgement.

Love/Affection: Don't go rushing into things or making any commitments which you might later regret. You've got plenty of time to think matters over and make sure that any decisions you make will be the right ones.

466 – HORSESHOE CROSSROADS FRUIT-TREE

General Situation: Any plans that you are making for home improvements or indeed a change of house should turn out well.

However, you may experience some preliminary setbacks. Don't let these put you off.

Finance/Business: This is a good time for taking some small financial risks but they must be small. Any scheme which could involve considerable financial outlay or perhaps even a second mortgage would not be advisable at present.

Love/Affection: You are in for a surprise and a very pleasant one at that. Your partner has been planning this treat for some time so make sure that you show your appreciation.

465 – HORSESHOE CROSSROADS GOBLET

General Situation: You will receive an invitation from a person you have only recently met. It will be to a social function of some kind, a party maybe. Go – it will really be an eye-opener.

Finance/Business: While it can be very pleasant to spend money on wining and dining occasionally, this is becoming rather a habit with you. Take a little more care of the pennies as you will need them to invest in something special very soon.

Love/Affection: For married couples, this will be a very happy period of your lives with plenty to do and plenty to celebrate. Single people could well meet someone over a casual drink who will become very important in their lives.

464 – HORSESHOE CROSSROADS KEY

General Situation: By a sheer stroke of good luck you will find yourself on the receiving end of an extremely good offer. This may cause friends to be jealous but it will solve a lot of your worries in one go.

Finance/Business: You will soon be able to purchase something which you have your heart set on and which you have been saving up for over the last few years. This extra money will come from a lottery, a small pools win or maybe even a lucky bet on the horses.

Love/Affection: You and your partner will be able to settle your differences at long last. Your relationship will become stronger and more permanent.

463 – HORSESHOE CROSSROADS LADDER

General Situation: Luck is with you at the moment and so are good health and ample energy. Now is the time to make any decisions which could prove to be turning points in your life. Depending on how you decide to do things, it could also see you climbing the ladder of success. Turn a chance event into an advantage.

Finance/Business: If you ever wanted to take a chance and hesitated before – don't hesitate now, gambles or risks are sure to pay off. A surprise promotion or increase of funds is also indicated.

Love/Affection: Everything in the garden is rosy – happiness, laughter and affection abound. For single people now is a good time to think about settling down and making plans for the future.

462 – HORSESHOE CROSSROADS LIGHTNING

General Situation: Something totally unforseen and unplanned for will spoil the arrangements which you have been making. Let it – you will soon realize that it was a blessing in disguise.

Finance/Business: Keep your eyes open for a member of a rival company or concern who could well be practising a little industrial espionage. It could be very annoying to find that your plans had been copied.

Love/Affection: Stop being so moody and brooding about an episode which, if not forgotten, has been forgiven. Shake yourself out of this depression and do something positive and decisive.

461 – HORSESHOE CROSSROADS SNAIL

General Situation: Patience is a virtue and one which you seem to be lacking. Don't fret so much about delays and hold-ups – they can work for you as well as against.

Finance/Business: If you have money which can be tied up for several years in a long-term investment without leaving you short of working capital then go ahead and invest. Short-term schemes, however, do not look so promising.

Love/Affection: 'Give and take' in a relationship is what keeps it going but you seem to have been taking more than your fair share. It is time to reverse this situation.

456 – HORSESHOE CAT FRUIT-TREE

General Situation: Anything which you chose to get involved in will prosper and will benefit both you and your family. A chance to try something completely new will also be to your advantage.

Finance/Business: The way things are going the Jones' will have to keep up with you. At long last you'll be able to afford to make some improvements to your home which will greatly increase its value.

Love/Affection: Stay just as you are – that's just how your partner and friends like you and why you're so happy and contented.

455 – HORSESHOE CAT GOBLET

General Situation: Now that you seem to have made the grade and all your interests are thriving you deserve a treat. So do your family who have stood by you in the past. Throw a party to say thank you or take them all out for a meal.

Finance/Business: It's not generally a good idea to invest in the entertainment industry but it could prove very profitable for you. You might even consider taking over a country pub with your family, or even running a little bistro in town.

Love/Affection: Some of that little windfall you have just received – or soon will – should be spent on your partner. You both deserve a night out.

454 – HORSESHOE CAT KEY

General Situation: A secret worry which you have been keeping from your family for some time will soon be solved by a stroke of good luck. Then you can be your old cheerful self again.

Finance/Business: Now is the time to improve your financial situation by expanding your business interests and branching out into something new. The onus is on you to take the initiative.

Love/Affection: If family worries and responsibilities have been weighing rather heavily on you, try to make time in your busy day when you and your partner can be alone together. You both need some time off to relax.

453 – HORSESHOE CAT LADDER

General Situation: The time is right to turn your hopes into realities. Move with the times and channel all that nervous energy of yours into reaching your goal. Don't wait for family approval – just go ahead.

Finance/Business: Your family and home will be the main drain on your finances in the coming months. However, whether you decide on a move of home, building an extension or just redecorating a room it will be money well spent which will bring pleasure to you all.

Love/Affection: If you've been letting yourself go a little, now is the time to smarten yourself up. Don't allow familiarity to breed contempt, your partner is sure to appreciate the effort.

452 – HORSESHOE CAT LIGHTNING

General Situation: Don't go bringing the wrath of your entire family down about your ears just because you've acted on the spur of the moment and made a foolish mistake. Discuss plans first and then everyone will stay happy.

Finance/Business: Don't risk all the capital that you've worked so hard to build up on a rush business deal or an impulse buy. You should be sure that you are in possession of all the facts and have had plenty of time for thought before you act.

Love/Affection: You should try to be a little more demonstrative towards your partner if you want to keep in their good books. A little present to show your appreciation might help to show that they're not taken too much for granted.

451 – HORSESHOE CAT SNAIL

General Situation: It's about time you took a break and gave yourself some time to think. A few days at home doing nothing would soon see you refreshed and raring to go again.

Finance/Business: Business matters should be thought over, carefully planned and then executed and not entered into on the spur of the moment without prior consideration. This can only lead you into problems.

Love/Affection: It wouldn't hurt to show your partner a little more affection or at least consideration. Don't overdo it, though, or they may think you're up to something.

446 – HORSESHOE KNIFE FRUIT-TREE

General Situation: Check out that your house and its contents are adequately insured. Also make sure that all your doors and windows are properly secured because there's a lot of petty theft about and you don't want to fall victim to it.

Finance/Business: Keep the details of your financial position to yourself. There are people around who are dishonest and may try to relieve you of some of your hard-earned money if they can get the chance.

Love/Affection: Is there a rival for your partner's affections? Do nothing for the moment as it may be quite harmless but be prepared to act should it be necessary.

445 – HORSESHOE KNIFE GOBLET

General Situation: Your outlook for the future seems to be set for success but don't go counting your chickens too soon, this is not yet the time for reckless spending. What could your friends be keeping from you?

Finance/Business: Business and pleasure really do not mix, especially at the moment – you should know this by now. They really must be kept separate if you want your plans to succeed.

Love/Affection: All these arguments must stop, these petty little jealousies and grumbles are not worth the fuss. No relationship is perfect and the sooner you realize it the sooner you will be able to put things on an even keel again.

444 – HORSESHOE KNIFE KEY

General Situation: You may not appreciate it now but that opportunity you missed was a blessing in disguise. It would have been a very risky venture. However, don't despair as a second chance is coming which will be very much more in your line.

Finance/Business: Watch out for friction at work between two of your workmates. Do your best to patch things up between them before their bickering upsets some of your well laid plans.

Love/Affection: The only good thing about arguments is making up afterwards. If you want to avoid arguments altogether try to be a little more open with your partner and explain to them what you have been planning.

443 – HORSESHOE KNIFE LADDER

General Situation: Generally things look very promising for you but it would not be a good idea to take too many risks or you could come unstuck. A little careful forward planning will help.

Finance/Business: A most unlikely person, one you never dreamed was on your side, will single you out for higher things. Make the most of this golden opportunity.

Love/Affection: You really must try to be a little more tolerant about your partner's shortcomings. Stop criticizing and be a little more helpful instead, it might make a difference.

442 – HORSESHOE KNIFE LIGHTNING

General Situation: If you wish to avoid annoying delays and setbacks try to curb your enthusiasm a little. Put those good ideas into action one step at a time after much careful thought and consideration. More haste – less speed!

Finance/Business: Your financial and business prospects look excellent. Don't go spoiling matters through over-hastiness or cutting corners.

Love/Affection: You may be feeling rather jealous because your partner seems to have so many commitments and interests which you don't share. Stop feeling so resentful and instead find something you can do together.

441 – HORSESHOE KNIFE SNAIL

General Situation: Problems concerning the care of an elderly relative will seem to be never-ending. Try not to let this become a drain on your own health and strength. Whenever you find you have some spare time use it to do something you want to do for a change.

Finance/Business: You have few money worries and problems at the moment. However, this doesn't mean that you can afford to go taking risks. Always think matters over carefully before you decide to take action.

Love/Affection: If your emotional life seems to have become a little stale and boring it could well be your own fault. Give it a stir and try something new.

436 – HORSESHOE HEART FRUIT-TREE

General Situation: This is a tremendous combination of symbols. Whatever you decide to do will be successful and you really can't go wrong. Enjoy it while it lasts.

Finance/Business: Now is the time to splash out and invest in a hobby or on some personal indulgence which you are unable to resist. Any money spent on the home and family will prove to be a good investment.

Love/Affection: This is your time when everything will be going for you. Make the most of it and really savour every moment.

435 – HORSESHOE HEART GOBLET

General Situation: This is a period with plenty to do and much to celebrate. Activities with friends or family are indicated.

Finance/Business: It's odd how things tend to snowball and this is just what's about to happen to you. Something which started off as a gamble will suddenly catch on and grow at an alarming speed.

Love/Affection: Try to forget about money for a while because this is a time for love and togetherness. The rat race will still be there waiting for you, but at the moment your relationship is more important.

434 – HORSESHOE HEART KEY

General Situation: By a sheer stroke of good luck you will get the opportunity to do something you've always dreamed of. Do it well and who knows where it could lead you.

Finance/Business: Long term plans will meet with the approval of a friend who has the right kind of influence to help promote them. This is an almost heaven-sent opportunity for you to break into new fields of activity.

Love/Affection: Your private life just couldn't be better, or could it? If you have plans or proposals to put to your partner concerning your future, now is the time to do it.

433 - HORSESHOE HEART LADDER

General Situation: By your own sheer hard work you will make great strides towards a personal goal. This will be a very rewarding experience although not necessarily in a momentary sense.

Finance/Business: The success of an important and, in the opinion of some people, rather an ambitious project is almost certainly assured. However, you must double-check that you have done your sums properly before embarking upon it.

Love/Affection: If your partner has had their heart set upon something which would undoubtedly give them great pleasure why not try to get it for them as a surprise. But only if it's financially possible.

432 - HORSESHOE HEART LIGHTNING

General Situation: Sudden good fortune from a most unexpected quarter will mean that you have to change some of your plans slightly. Make sure that your family understand what you're trying to do or friction could result.

Finance/Business: Although generally not a good idea, you could make an exception this time and have a little flutter on the horses especially on one named after a member of your family. But don't make it a habit.

Love/Affection: An impulsive action on your part could bring a little sparkle back into your life. It will bring enjoyment to you and your partner and a few surprises too.

431 - HORSESHOE HEART SNAIL

General Situation: Luck seems to be smiling on you and the Midas touch will be much in evidence in everything you do. Matters of the heart are also well aspected and you will be surrounded by love and affection. However, watch your health! Don't take liberties and burn the candle at both ends. Good luck and love won't do you much good if you're feeling too tired to enjoy them.

Finance/Business: Provided that you avoid making silly and hurried decisions, nothing much can go wrong at present. Not only will your plans be successful but you have the backing and help of colleagues as well. It may even be worth taking a business risk provided that you calculate the odds carefully at first.

Love/Affection: A happy, loving time with your family. Between you and your partner, love will be given as well as received just when you were thinking things had gone a little flat. Much laughter and happiness.

426 – HORSESHOE STORK FRUIT-TREE

General Situation: You will shortly be entering into a very creative phase in your life when you should promote any new ideas you may have, however revolutionary they may seem. Some are sure to bear fruit.

Finance/Business: Your main problem during the coming period will be finding the time to benefit from some of the money you'll be so busy earning. You'll also have the pleasure of saying that 'it's all my own work'.

Love/Affection: You and your partner should pool your resources. Your combined talents, if channelled in the right direction, make a formidable union.

425 – HORSESHOE STORK GOBLET

General Situation: If you haven't got anything in particular to celebrate then you must just sit down and invent something. This is no time for staying at home.

Finance/Business: Don't give up now and throw the towel in if some venture isn't going quite to plan. Re-think the situation and perhaps after one or two minor modifications you'll be ready to go. A breakthrough is coming.

Love/Affection: All in all this will be a hectic but enjoyable time.

424 – HORSESHOE STORK KEY

General Situation: You are in for a run of good luck which is long overdue.

Finance/Business: Before taking advantage of a very generous offer, it would be sensible to study all the implications. If you doubt your own business sense, then seek expert advice.

Love/Affection: This time you're on your own and your partner can't help you except by being a good listener as and when you need one. Take advantage of this.

423 – HORSESHOE STORK LADDER

General Situation: Good luck together with creative ability will enable you to achieve a special ambition. Careful planning is the key as without this problems could occur.

Finance/Business: In order to build up some capital, it may be necessary to take the odd calculated risk or two. Your rather tenuous plans need a little more thought before they can be considered viable.

Love/Affection: You two really do need some sort of target or ambition to channel your energies into, instead of just sitting around feeling bored. Put your heads together and see what you can come up with.

422 – HORSESHOE STORK LIGHTNING

General Situation: This is a creative time when you will be required to work under pressure. Enter into things wholeheartedly as there can be no half measures. You may not gain financially from this but your reputation will certainly be enhanced.

Finance/Business: Try not to make your 'ambitious streak' quite so obvious. There is someone in a senior position who may be worried for his own job and who may resort to a few cunning tricks to make sure that you remain where you are.

Love/Affection: Although you may find a colleague of the opposite sex extremely attractive, this should stay a case of worship from afar. Don't do anything precipitous or you might regret it.

421 – HORSESHOE STORK SNAIL

General Situation: You must take more care of yourself. Go to bed early for a change. You can't expect peak performance when you neglect yourself.

Finance/Business: Don't allow family pressure to coerce you into buying something rather expensive for the home on the spur of the moment. If you take time to shop around you'll be surprised how much prices differ from shop to shop.

Love/Affection: Spend some time alone with your partner and use this time to formulate a few long-term plans.

416 – HORSESHOE SUN FRUIT-TREE

General Situation: Your outlook for the future just couldn't be better. Dreams should soon become realities and you should be feeling very pleased with yourself. You will be feeling in peak condition and raring to go. Enjoy yourself.

Finance/Business: This will be a time of plenty, when not only will you be able to make ends meet without a struggle but you will also have some surplus cash to spend on the home or other interests. Promotion at work is indicated.

Love/Affection: Keep an eye on any joint accounts as your partner may have been overspending in an attempt to keep up with the Jones's. It would be a good idea to review your financial position together so that you both know how much you can afford to spend on luxuries.

415 – HORSESHOE SUN GOBLET

General Situation: Through a stroke of good fortune a rather risky scheme will actually come off.

Finance/Business: A rather interesting business proposition could be put to you over a meal. However, find out a little more about it before making any commitment – the wine may have gone to your head.

Love/Affection: It's no good saying that you never meet anyone new when you don't go anywhere. Get out and about a bit more or even throw a party of your own. Do something positive.

414 – HORSESHOE SUN KEY

General Situation: Don't allow your family and friends to ride rough-shod over you. Be more assertive and make them do what you want just for once. Don't become a 'yes' man or woman just for the sake of a little peace and quiet.

Finance/Business: It will be necessary to delegate more in order to get through your increasingly heavy workload. This will also enable you to gain a little more time to spend on a rather ambitious and complicated venture of your own.

Love/Affection: A change of partner is indicated which will be relatively easy to accomplish for single people. Think matters over with great care before arriving at any decision.

413 – HORSESHOE SUN LADDER

General Situation: Lady Luck has decided to smile on you so you will have little trouble getting whatever you want no matter how ambitious it may seem. Make the most of your opportunities and above all enjoy your success.

Finance/Business: What a success story yours will be as long as you keep your head and remain firmly in control of the situation. Take the plunge and go all out for success – you're sure to reach the top.

Love/Affection: You and your partner make a formidable team and provided that you pull together you will achieve a great deal.

412 – HORSESHOE SUN LIGHTNING

General Situation: An impulsive action could well start a whole new way of life for you and it will set into motion a chain of events that you had not bargained for. Go ahead – leap before you look for a change.

Finance/Business: If you are ambitious and want to get on in life then this could be the right time to consider changing your career. Seek a position with more responsibility and greater scope for advancement.

Love/Affection: Whatever it was you did to make your partner so indignant you had better hurry up and make amends somehow.

The longer you leave it the harder it will be to restore peace and harmony to your relationship.

411 – HORSESHOE SUN SNAIL

General Situation: You've had a busy time lately and have much to be thankful for. Allow yourself a little more time to relax and count your blessings. Don't forget to thank those who gave you a helping hand.

Finance/Business: Use this slack period to catch up on all your paper-work, but be careful what you write, especially if filling in tax forms or legal documents. You must make things quite clear or misunderstandings will occur.

Love/Affection: You both deserve a holiday so take a break from that hectic life of yours when you seem to be constantly working against time to get things done. A little time together with nothing to do would be a pleasant change.

366 – BOAT CROSSROADS FRUIT-TREE

General Situation: Don't be surprised if you are suddenly required to pack your bags and rush off somewhere. You will find that this will result in some kind of personal gain although it may not be just money.

Finance/Business: The outcome of a report at work will really put the cat amongst the pigeons and will leave one or two people with rather red faces – make sure that you are not one of them. Auditors can uncover all sorts of errors.

Love/Affection: It's about time you made a few new friends in your neighbourhood. Someone you will meet at a social function will have a great influence on your plans for the future.

365 – BOAT CROSSROADS GOBLET

General Situation: A letter is coming which will contain some rather unexpected news. You will have to revise a few plans and perhaps cancel one or two engagements in order to gain time to consider the matter.

Finance/Business: A business contact which you made some time ago, and never got around to following up, will be re-established through an unexpected telephone call. Don't lose touch this time or you will miss an important lead.

Love/Affection: Oh dear! Someone from your dark and murky past is about to make an unexpected re-appearance. Watch out for quarrels and jealousy.

364 – BOAT CROSSROADS KEY

General Situation: During the coming period you will receive many interesting and varied offers and you will find it hard to decide which one to follow up. You could even get the chance to travel so make sure that your passport is up-to-date.

Finance/Business: Keep an eye on strangers who you feel are somehow rather suspicious, particularly if you are going away for any period of time and will be leaving your property unattended. Double check that all doors and windows are safely secured.

Love/Affection: Watch out for someone who has recently joined your circle of friends. They may see you as the answer to all their problems and could spring one or two nasty surprises.

363 – BOAT CROSSROADS LADDER

General Situation: If you are at all ambitious follow up a surprise opportunity which will come your way – it could lead to bigger things and at the very least will be most enjoyable.

Finance/Business: Now is the time to check up on what business rivals are up to – you could be in for a bit of a shock. Get out and about more and do some research in the field if you want to stay abreast of current trends.

Love/Affection: Nothing ventured – nothing gained. Try to put matters right between you and your partner with a telephone call or even a little present. You have reached a crossroads in your relationship and it's up to you to decide which path you want to take.

362 – BOAT CROSSROADS LIGHTNING

General Situation: This is a time for action and you should get on the move. Why not pay a surprise visit to some friends or relatives that you haven't seen for some time. Failing that there must be some letters you should have written or telephone calls you should have made.

Finance/Business: Don't allow an increase in your workload to make you careless. You must not be tempted to rush a job and turn out a second-rate performance. Be prepared for a letter bearing some unexpected news.

Love/Affection: Don't be too quick off the mark to blame your partner if one or two things start to go wrong. It could be your fault. You must be more tolerant and patient.

361 – BOAT CROSSROADS SNAIL

General Situation: If you are planning any journeys, no matter how short, be prepared for hold-ups and delays. In fact it would be a good idea to set off a little earlier than necessary just in case.

Finance/Business: This is not a good time to go taking any risks either business-wise or with your own money. You would be better advised to mark time for a while until the economic situation improves. Instead, use this time to formulate new plans which can be implemented later.

Love/Affection: Try not to do anything foolish in front of strangers or your partner may be embarrassed and annoyed by your behaviour. Think before you act.

356 – BOAT CAT FRUIT-TREE

General Situation: A piece of information that you will receive from a close relative or in-law will be of considerable interest to you. If you act wisely you should be able to benefit from it.

Finance/Business: Make a very careful check of your finances as you might find that you have been overcharged for something you have recently purchased. Also make sure that an important letter hasn't gone unnoticed or unanswered. It could save you money.

Love/Affection: Day-dreaming about what might be is all very well in its place but your constant head in the clouds attitude could be very irritating for your partner. If you've been fantasizing over a holiday abroad or a better house, do something positive about it for a change.

355 – BOAT CAT GOBLET

General Situation: There couldn't be a better time to enjoy yourself than now. But don't just do it alone, make sure that you include your family too. Plan a get-together, a weekend away or even a night out at the cinema or a local restaurant – you'll all be sure to have a good time.

Finance/Business: Good news is on the way that will benefit both you and your family financially and socially. Something which you had previously thought impossible can now be done with relative ease.

Love/Affection: Be prepared – your social life is about to go into top gear. Lots of new and exciting people to meet and fun things to do. Foreign travel is also indicated.

354 – BOAT CAT KEY

General Situation: Life really can be what you decide to make of it as you have everything going for you just now – opportunities, lucky chances, family backing and approval. You have a free hand so play it carefully and you should not go wrong.

Finance/Business: Your business outlook for the coming period seems excellent. However, in order to take full advantage of chances that will arise you must be prepared to make a sacrifice of some kind which could prove a difficult decision for you.

Love/Affection: Any change in your partner, however slight, whether in attitude or in appearance, should not go unnoticed by you. Talk about it as there is a definite reason for this change.

353 – BOAT CAT LADDER

General Situation: If you are ambitious, opportunity won't come looking for you at home. You must be prepared to get out and about and make yourself known to people. The potential is there if only you use it.

Finance/Business: It might be a good idea to see if your family would be willing to back you financially in a new project that you want to get off the ground. Don't be too proud to ask.

Love/Affection: Your family will be very much involved in your personal affairs one way or another over this coming period. But remember that there are some things that are best kept to yourself.

352 – BOAT CAT LIGHTNING

General Situation: If you make any spur-of-the-moment plans for a holiday or an outing you could find yourself in hot water with those around you who may have different ideas. Talk things over with them.

Finance/Business: If a relative or in-law comes to you with a request for some kind of financial assistance you should treat this matter with great care. A quixotic gesture on your part could be the start of something you will later regret.

Love/Affection: Do something impulsive. Take your partner completely by surprise with an un-birthday present or have a night out to celebrate the cat's birthday. Anything will do so long as it is out of the ordinary.

351 – BOAT CAT SNAIL

General Situation: A break in the sun could be just what you need to help you relax and regain some of your energy. Get away from your home and family if only for a few days to give yourself time to think. If you really can't get away then take the phone off the hook and try to forget about everything for a while.

Finance/Business: Take great care if you have to sign any legal documents, especially if they involve your house or personal possessions. If there is something which you don't understand you must make it your business to find out. And if there is anything which you don't like the look of, then ask for extra time to mull things over. Avoid hurried decisions!

Love/Affection: Try not to make any hasty plans where your private life is concerned. Think matters over very carefully and make sure that you are in full possession of all the facts before reaching a decision.

346 – BOAT KNIFE FRUIT-TREE

General Situation: It would be advisable to double-check any plans you have made through a third-party – especially where travel arrangements are concerned. A telephone call now could save you a lot of trouble and embarrassment later on.

Finance/Business: Avoid delegating responsibilities which are really yours as other people may not be quite so conscientious as you. There is a colleague who would be only too glad to see you make a mistake.

Love/Affection: Make sure that any messages or notes you may leave for your partner are crystal clear or you may return to find yourself in their bad books. A little more thoughtfulness on your part could avoid unnecessary arguments.

345 – BOAT KNIFE GOBLET

General Situation: A surprise invitation to party or celebration may not be as innocuous as it first seems. If you decide to accept you must remember to keep your wits about you or you may be deceived.

Finance/Business: Pay careful attention to the menu when dining out with a business associate or client. Stick to what you know especially if ordering foreign food.

Love/Affection: If communications between you and your partner seem to have broken down slightly and have become rather monosyllabic, why not have a quiet meal out and patch things up. You can't solve a problem until you have talked things over and found the cause.

344 – BOAT KNIFE KEY

General Situation: You should think very carefully before embarking on any new undertaking, especially if it appears to be a heaven-sent opportunity to solve a few personal problems. It is far easier to fail than to succeed, so don't leave anything to chance.

Finance/Business: Now would be a very good time to consider a change of job, especially if you have been working for a very politically-structured organization. Don't do anything precipitous but be on the look-out for an opening elsewhere.

Love/Affection: Holiday romances are all very well and can be great fun if you don't allow yourself to become too involved. Just as you might put on an act away from home to impress another, so can someone else. Don't be made to look a fool.

343 – BOAT KNIFE LADDER

General Situation: Play things very close to your chest, especially where your personal ambitions are concerned. Once you let another into your confidence you run the risk of having your plans spoilt.

Finance/Business: When taking a gamble, especially with your own money, make sure that you really can afford to lose. New projects can cost a great deal of money to set up so don't be in too much of a hurry to invest and don't believe everything you're told. Check things out for yourself first.

Love/Affection: In a personal relationship you must be prepared to make your feelings known even if this does spark off arguments and quarrels. Try not to be timid, you must clear the air to find out if what exists between you is really worth having or whether your relationship has just become a habit.

342 – BOAT KNIFE LIGHTNING

General Situation: As the result of a letter or telephone call, it will soon be necessary for you to make a journey. You will probably find this irritating but the journey is vital.

Finance/Business: Due to problems with business communications, it may be necessary for you to make a number of short journeys. Be prepared to meet unwelcome people on your travels.

Love/Affection: Avoid misleading someone. Make sure that you really know what you want. It would be thoughtless and unfeeling to let them down at the last moment because you change your mind.

341 – BOAT KNIFE SNAIL

General Situation: You must try to slow your pace if you don't want your health to suffer from overwork. Try to plan your workload so that you don't have to make more journeys than necessary. Don't be tricked into doing something which you really think is beyond your capabilities.

Finance/Business: This is a time to be like the ostrich and keep your head well down – if not actually buried. Avoid the temptation to invest money, however small an amount, even if the scheme looks like a winner.

Love/Affection: Try not to let your restlessness irritate your partner. This period will soon pass and you should concentrate on relaxing together and generally taking things a little easier.

336 – BOAT HEART FRUIT-TREE

General Situation: Now could be a good time to take a sentimental journey and visit old friends and old places. You might even learn something about yourself.

Finance/Business: If you or your firm have any money tied up in foreign investments it would be a good idea to keep a close eye on the political situations of the countries in question. Be prepared to either withdraw or invest quickly, once you have assessed the situation.

Love/Affection: If you want to create a good impression with your partner or a loved one, now is the time to spend a little money on them as a show of your appreciation.

335 – BOAT HEART GOBLET

General Situation: It should now be possible for you to achieve something which you had hitherto thought impossible. Someone influential should be instrumental in this. Watch the post.

Finance/Business: A rather successful business venture in which you are involved will give you much cause to celebrate. But don't take all the glory for yourself.

Love/Affection: Avoid getting too involved in your own triumphs and achievements so that you forget to include your partner in your success.

334 – BOAT HEART KEY

General Situation: An opportunity could arise which might bring a solution to a problem which has been worrying you. This opportunity might be revealed after receiving a letter. A change of home is also a possibility. This is something you have wanted for some time.

Finance/Business: A busy time ahead with many letters to be written and telephone calls to be made. An opening could arise which will give you the opportunity to combine both business and pleasure. It could even be a change of job.

Love/Affection: A trip to see relatives who live some distance away and the chance to sort out family problems face-to-face will probably result from a message. Don't keep old misunderstandings to yourself. Air your grievances as you may have the wrong impression.

333 – BOAT HEART LADDER

General Situation: This is a good time to visit family or friends who live abroad. Apart from enjoying yourself, it might give you some insight into the way other people tackle various problems. And this might help you at a later date.

Finance/Business: Although this could be a very eventful period for you with new projects to be launched, try not to neglect your loved ones. If you have to stay away from home for any length of time, remember to keep in touch.

Love/Affection: It is quite possible that on your travels you will make an important new friendship. This would be worth cultivating and could be of help to you in the future.

332 – BOAT HEART LIGHTNING

General Situation: Some information you will receive about a friend should be taken with a pinch of salt. Messages sometimes have a habit of getting distorted and it would be a shame to spoil a good friendship through a misunderstanding.

Finance/Business: Should you have to be absent from work or home for a period, make sure that you have appointed a friend or member of your family to delegate for you. An important letter or telephone call may require immediate action.

Love/Affection: You must remember to keep your partner up to date with any plans you are making, especially if they involve travel. You may be regarded with suspicion if you go rushing off somewhere without a word of warning.

331 – BOAT HEART SNAIL

General Situation: If you are feeling tired and want a day or two to relax, don't let friends talk you into doing something strenuous.

Finance/Business: Don't allow personal feelings to cloud a financial decision you will have to make. Study all the facts very carefully and pay attention to small print.

Love/Affection: Unavoidable delays may prevent you from being on time when meeting your partner for a special occasion. Try to get a message through somehow.

326 – BOAT STORK FRUIT-TREE

General Situation: A new baby coming into your family will be prosperous and much travelled in later life. An idea of your own which you are trying to promote could well prove to be a money-spinner abroad. Put pen to paper and make enquiries about overseas outlets.

Finance/Business: In order to solve financial problems it might be necessary to go back to square one and do some rethinking. New ideas or a new approach are necessary if you want to get out of (and stay out of) the red.

Love/Affection: If you and your partner want to keep your relationship happy and fulfilling then avoid arguments over money at all costs. By all means discuss financial matters but always on a friendly basis – if you don't then you could find yourselves parting company.

325 – BOAT STORK GOBLET

General Situation: Life for you is going to be busy and full of fun. However, don't go discussing your ideas and future intentions with strangers. No matter how good the company and how chatty you are feeling, keep your own business very much to yourself. Careless talk could cost you your ideas.

Finance/Business: The best time for you to get over new ideas and proposals would be at a business luncheon or over drinks after work with either your boss, your colleagues or an important client. It could provide just the opportunity you have been waiting for.

Love/Affection: Your partner could well try to sweet-talk you into something. Go along with their plan.

324 – BOAT STORK KEY

General Situation: The chance will arise to try something creative and completely outside your normal range of activities. Have a go – you could be pleasantly surprised by the outcome.

Finance/Business: Workwise it looks as if you will be in for a very busy and eventful time. New doors will be opening for you but it's up to you to make sure they stay open. You will only succeed through your own efforts. Foreign travel is also indicated.

Love/Affection: It seems likely that someone new will come into your life whom you will find both different and stimulating. This could be just the chance you have been waiting for.

323 – BOAT STORK LADDER

General Situation: Write a few letters or telephone around to see if you can find someone who would be interested in your ideas. You won't get anywhere if you don't try, so sell yourself more.

Finance/Business: If business seems a little slow in this country, then why not make enquiries to see if you might do better for yourself abroad. If you are ambitious then you should be prepared to go where the best prospects are.

Love/Affection: Your present relationship seems to have stagnated so it's up to you to decide whether to cut your losses or whether to try again. If you do opt for a second chance, then try to show a little more enthusiasm and be generally more demonstrative.

322 – BOAT STORK LIGHTNING

General Situation: Avoid writing letters or making telephone calls in anger. Try to find out what has gone wrong. You could discover that plans have not been properly explained to you and that once you are in the picture all will be well.

Finance/Business: This would be a good time to have all electrical appliances and communications equipment such as telephones and telexes at work checked out. Look out your service agreements and get this done swiftly. You may be quite shocked by the engineers' findings.

Love/Affection: You and your partner should start thinking very seriously about your plans for the future. However, before you embark on anything new, take sufficient time to talk things over and to view your ideas from all angles. Make some written notes if it helps.

321 – BOAT STORK SNAIL

General Situation: Any important decisions you have to make will keep for the time being. The most important thing to do is to restore yourself to peak condition, perhaps a general medical examination would set your mind at rest.

Finance/Business: It's a good time to visit the trade shows, seminars and meetings in your particular industry or field. Keep your eyes open for new approaches to old problems and bear these in mind for future reference. Don't be tempted to invest any money at the moment – look, learn but don't buy.

Love/Affection: Where your private life is concerned, your probable best course of action would be to stay at home with some good books to read or catch up on any outstanding correspondence. Don't do anything on impulse as your ideas are unlikely to come to anything at the moment.

316 – BOAT SUN FRUIT-TREE

General Situation: Good news from abroad could brighten up your life and could even be the reason for you having to do some travelling later in the year. Start saving up now.

Finance/Business: A complete reshuffle at work looks likely when all the dead wood will be pruned out quite savagely. However, there's no need for you to worry as this will leave the way clear for you to rise a little higher up the ladder. If you are offered the chance to invest in your firm then take it.

Love/Affection: A cheerful, happy, harmonious time ahead for you if you're married. And if you happen to be single then watch out as someone new and very special is about to enter your life.

315 – BOAT SUN GOBLET

General Situation: Try being a little more cheerful and personable – it could help in more ways than one.

Finance/Business: If you really want to succeed and get on in this world you must try to be more forceful and decisive. Stop wishing for the impossible and instead channel your energies into projects which are within your capabilities. Success can be yours if you could only be more realistic.

Love/Affection: Some good news that you and your partner will receive will spur you on to attempt something you have both been contemplating for some time now. This calls for a celebration.

314 – BOAT SUN KEY

General Situation: You probably have worries and problems. These won't solve themselves so you must seize every opportunity you can find to put matters right. This will probably be very time-consuming but once you have things back on an even keel again you'll be glad you bothered.

Finance/Business: Promotion and more responsibility will come your way very soon. This opportunity could also involve a great deal of travelling which you may not want. Think very carefully before reaching a decision as you won't be asked a second time.

Love/Affection: It may be necessary for you and your partner to be separated for a while should you decide to take a job away from home. Don't worry too much as you are sure to make a success of things and you'll be re-united very soon.

313 – BOAT SUN LADDER

General Situation: A journey which you make for pleasure will have a few pleasant surprises for you. You will return full of enthusiasm and with many new ideas you will want to put into action immediately.

Finance/Business: If you have been thinking of moving home and investigating in a bigger or better property then this could be the right time to make the move.

Love/Affection: If you and your partner have ever discussed going into business together and never got round to doing anything about it, then you should start rethinking again, right now. It could be the best move you are likely to make.

312 – BOAT SUN LIGHTNING

General Situation: Don't allow a misunderstanding between you and a friend to get out of proportion. Instead of sitting and brooding about it, go and see them immediately to put matters right.

Finance/Business: Take great care to avoid any accidents at work which could result from a lapse in concentration. Be especially careful if driving a firm's car or when travelling to or from a business appointment.

Love/Affection: This should be a very rewarding time for both you and your partner when there will be much to do and many arrangements to make. You should also derive tremendous pleasure from each other's company, when a greater harmony and understanding will develop.

311 – BOAT SUN SNAIL

General Situation: You seem to be filled with an almost overwhelming desire to travel but this may not be possible because of obstacles you will encounter which will prohibit your movements. You could be extremely glad later on that you remained.

Finance/Business: You may find that your telephone and postage bills are unusually high over the next few months but this is a necessary expenditure which will help you to pull off an ambitious venture that you have had in mind for some time. One word of warning though – make sure that you make yourself fully understood.

Love/Affection: Try not to be so full of yourself and your own importance that you don't take interest in your partner's ideas and plans. Pay them a little more attention, make sure that you listen to what they have to say and, above all – don't interrupt.

266 – SKULL CROSSROADS FRUIT-TREE

General Situation: If you have recently moved (or are about to) to a new locality then watch out for someone who appears over-friendly. Don't go telling them about your business or you could find them stirring up trouble for both you and your family.

Finance/Business: Financially, you could be faced with a decision you must make. Should you spend some money on the house you now live in or should you move to somewhere bigger and better, let your family help you to make up your mind.

Love/Affection: Don't allow an outsider to stir up trouble between you and your partner. They may have some unpleasant things to say, but try not to over-react to them. Think matters over and don't go making hasty moves.

265 – SKULL CROSSROADS GOBLET

General Situation: Gatecrashers at a party could cause trouble, and what was supposed to be a happy occasion for you and your friends could turn into chaos. Check your guest list very carefully and don't admit strangers.

Finance/Business: You could be in for some changes at work which you had least expected. An outsider, maybe an auditor or a new member of staff could create problems given half a chance. Watch out that your name doesn't appear on a redundancy list.

Love/Affection: Don't feel so safe and smug in your relationship as you do or you could be in for a bit of an eye-opener from a meddling neighbour. Pull your socks up and try to correct some of your worst faults.

264 – SKULL CROSSROADS KEY

General Situation: If you are at all worried about your health you would be well advised to see your GP and let him check things out for you – you are probably worrying yourself over nothing. Your family may be helpful and supportive but they are not qualified to make a diagnosis.

Finance/Business: An unexpected benefactor could arrive just in time to save you from a financially difficult situation. Learn from your mistakes and don't let yourself slide back into the same rut in another few months' time – you may not be so lucky again.

Love/Affection: Don't allow your family to meddle in your private affairs; what goes on between you and your partner is really none of their business. Ignore their attempts to influence you and follow your own feelings.

263 – SKULL CROSSROADS LADDER

General Situation: Don't allow the thought of failure to enter your mind if you embark upon something new. There's nothing you can't achieve when you really put your mind to it.

Finance/Business: If you really are hell-bent to try out something rather unheard of which you believe could change your lifestyle, then have a go. The choice is yours but don't allow other people with few ideas of their own to put you off.

Love/Affection: You are in for a very pleasant surprise which will leave you speechless for a while. Enjoy it while it lasts as it will be transitory and you will then have to come down to earth again.

262 – SKULL CROSSROADS LIGHTNING

General Situation: If you are considering sharing accommodation with someone, or maybe taking a lodger or students into your home, then think this step through very carefully indeed. Your peaceful day-to-day routine could be thrown into chaos and there's nothing like an outsider in the house to build up disagreements and disputes.

Finance/Business: Now is the time to check that all your insurance premiums have been paid up to date (it's quite easy to overlook such matters) and to ensure that your property and possessions are adequately covered for any contingency. Pay special note to the risk of fire and storm damage.

Love/Affection: If your partner seems to be spending a lot more time in front of the mirror lately and spending considerably more time over dress and appearance, don't immediately suspect them of having someone else. They are only doing it to please you at best and at worst they are starting to feel their age or trying to get out of a rut. Relax and stop worrying.

261 – SKULL CROSSROADS SNAIL

General Situation: Life is about to throw you in at the deep end with a whole series of changes which you had not bargained for. Don't worry – you'll be able to cope perfectly well as long as you watch what you're doing and don't allow anyone else to interfere.

Finance/Business: Financially your watchword over the coming months should be 'thrift'. Try to put some money away which will give you security and don't make any major purchases unless it is really necessary.

Love/Affection: A very persuasive stranger may try to steal your affections and this could cause no end of trouble if you allow them to turn your head. Look very carefully before you leap and consider the consequences!

256 – SKULL CAT FRUIT-TREE

General Situation: A long-standing health problem will soon be resolved, perhaps by some new form of treatment but more probably by seeking some form of alternative medicine which could prove costly but effective. Don't begrudge the cost – your health is important.

Finance/Business: Your property represents a very large capital asset as well as a home for you and your family. It needs looking after and now would be a good time to undertake repairs or improvements which are necessary.

Love/Affection: You and your partner could suddenly find yourselves going up in the world with more money to spend on yourselves and your surroundings. This could result from a win of some kind (pools, lottery), but probably from an inheritance.

255 – SKULL CAT GOBLET

General Situation: A wedding in the family could come as quite a surprise. Whoever it is, this announcement will bring some changes to your own life and something which you previously thought impossible can now be achieved.

Finance/Business: A family celebration (wedding/reunion) could see you dipping a little deeper into your pocket than you had anticipated. However, don't go getting yourself into debt over it and try to enjoy yourself – after all, you're paying for it.

Love/Affection: If you are still single then all that could be changing rapidly for you. If, however, you are already married then watch out for very pleasant and totally unexpected changes in your relationship. A good time for all, whatever their marital status.

254 – SKULL CAT KEY

General Situation: A new phase in your life is about to begin very soon which will affect not only you but your family as well. Old problems will be resolved and you will be able to start afresh with few personal worries to hold you back.

Finance/Business: Unexpected financial help from a distant relative couldn't come at a better time. This should enable you not only to pay off any outstanding debts but also to enter into a new venture.

Love/Affection: You and your partner will be offered the chance to try something you have always dreamed of. It's the tonic your relationship has been needing and will alter the views and feelings of you both quite dramatically.

253 – SKULL CAT LADDER

General Situation: A personal ambition may have to be postponed or put aside altogether because of a frustrating health problem or the conflicting plans of a relative. Don't brood about it too much, as you will get another chance and sooner than you think.

Finance/Business: Before dismissing an unexpected opportunity out of hand, just take a little time to think it over first. You could do it if you were sufficiently determined and it would certainly give you a boost. The choice is yours.

Love/Affection: If your partner seems indecisive about something out of the ordinary you might have suggested, make sure that they have completely come round to your way of thinking before you take any positive steps. You could fail without their backing.

252 – SKULL CAT LIGHTNING

General Situation: Any changes in your home or family life which you are planning to make shouldn't be embarked upon until you have given the idea a great deal of consideration. If you don't look at it from everyone's point of view you could make somebody very resentful and irritated.

Finance/Business: Don't take risks, however good the odds may seem at the time. You could lose everything you have worked so hard for, just because you acted impulsively and without care.

Love/Affection: Should your partner decide to turn down an opportunity which, on the face of it, looks very good, don't lose your temper. Once you know all the facts you'll be more understanding.

251 – SKULL CAT SNAIL

General Situation: Should you suddenly decide to throw yourself into a vigorous keep-fit campaign, don't be surprised if you pull a muscle or do some permanent damage. Take things gently.

Finance/Business: Avoid the temptation to make any impulsive buys. If you bother to ask around there's probably someone in your family who has just the thing you want and would be only too glad to give it to you.

Love/Affection: Avoid making waves in your private life. Your partner may not appreciate making changes if you haven't really thought things over first. Play safe.

246 – SKULL KNIFE FRUIT-TREE

General Situation: Now is the time to stop drifting. Get yourself a positive goal to work towards and really make an effort.

Finance/Business: Money worries and mounting bills may have been putting you under considerable strain lately but don't despair, there are changes coming soon which will solve all this. Keep your eyes open and pay special attention to the 'Situations Vacant' page of your local or trade newspaper.

Love/Affection: Someone with money to burn will try to turn your partner's head with expensive gifts and presents. Resist the urge to go looking for trouble, this will only make matters worse. Play it cool – it will die a natural death very soon when the money runs out.

245 – SKULL KNIFE GOBLET

General Situation: Don't allow old family feuds to spoil a get-together which is coming soon, especially if this is a wedding. Instead, why not forget the past, you can all afford to relax then and enjoy yourselves without the constant threat of arguments.

Finance/Business: Money really isn't everything. If you feel tempted to dabble in some dubious deals in order to make extra money, stop and ask yourself if it is really worth the risk. Do you really want that kind of worry hanging over you?

Love/Affection: If a silly quarrel with your partner over money is allowed to get out of hand then you really could have problems. Do everything you can to put matters right. If you have any little confessions to make, then make them now before the whole affair gets out of hand.

244 – SKULL KNIFE KEY

General Situation: It might be a good idea to break away from your present circle of friends and seek new company and interests elsewhere. These people are not very loyal and would leave you in the lurch only too readily, should you no longer be of use to them.

Finance/Business: Don't get involved in any get-rich-quick schemes, however good they sound. There's usually a catch somewhere.

Love/Affection: Try not to let jealousy spoil your relationship as undoubtedly it will if you continually try to catch your partner out. You must make the effort and try to be more trusting in future.

243 – SKULL KNIFE LADDER

General Situation: When embarking on any new projects, first make sure that you really do understand what you are doing and how everything works, especially if this involves using machinery with which you are not familiar. If you remember to put safety first you won't go far wrong.

Finance/Business: Entering into a partnership with a friend might not be such a good idea as it seems. It is better to retain control yourself even if this does mean stretching your finances to the limit.

Love/Affection: You two really must sort out your problems if your relationship is to last. Quarrelling and arguments are not doing either of you any good. Try to communicate more and make any changes, however drastic, that will improve the situation.

242 – SKULL KNIFE LIGHTNING

General Situation: You will have to move fast and do some even faster talking to get yourself out of a mess you could find yourself in. Unfortunately, it's likely to be your own fault. However, it's not too late to reform.

Finance/Business: When faced at work with something unexpected, and not really to your liking, don't over-react and refuse point blank to tackle the problem. A foolish argument now could lead to serious difficulties.

Love/Affection: Your private life is in for a few storms. You are both going to have to iron out one or two problems which cause arguments and if a compromise isn't possible then you could find yourselves going your own separate ways.

241 – SKULL KNIFE SNAIL

General Situation: If the worries and problems of everyday life are really beginning to get you down, then do something about it now before your health starts to deteriorate. Get away for a few days, maybe to friends or relatives, where you can relax. A change and a rest will do you good.

Finance/Business: You should shop around if you intend to purchase an expensive item such as a motor car, stereo unit, video, etc. This way you will not only be able to see all the models available but get the best price too.

Love/Affection: If your personal affairs are in a bit of a turmoil, try not to do anything on the spur of the moment. This could only make matters worse. Don't discuss your problems with anyone – especially not a close friend.

236 – SKULL HEART FRUIT-TREE

General Situation: Life for you is going to change for the better – quite unexpectedly and sooner than you think. Be prepared for a new job, a change in residence, more money, new friends or a new love in your life. The change could be just one or more of these.

Finance/Business: You seem to be possessed of the Midas touch at the moment. Not only do you attract money but you have the necessary knowledge, experience and intuition to use it wisely and make it work for you. This ability could lead to new and exciting job prospects.

Love/Affection: A new and important person will enter your life and friendship will blossom into something deeper. Just one word of warning – is it you they really admire or all the things you have like money, possessions, influence?

235 – SKULL HEART GOBLET

General Situation: A chance is coming for you to do something you have always dreamed about. This opportunity will be closely connected with an old family friend and will have far-reaching consequences.

Finance/Business: Try not to overspend on frivolous pleasures or you could find that, when you are most in need of some money, there is none left.

Love/Affection: Your private life is not going to be quite so private during the next few weeks and you and your partner will be spending a lot of time in the company of others. This will be a busy time for you both.

234 – SKULL HEART KEY

General Situation: Don't let a sudden change in your life catch you out. Instead, make it work for you and turn the situation into a personal triumph. You will surprise both yourself and your friends by the way you handle the matter.

Finance/Business: If offered a new job some distance from home, perhaps even in another country, think very carefully before reaching a decision. You must weigh the pros and cons – the income may well be higher than your present salary but are you prepared to leave your loved ones in order to enjoy it?

Love/Affection: Cheer up – as one door closes another one opens, and that is just what's going to happen for you. Forget the past and instead look forward to the future. You will soon be finding someone new to share it with.

233 – SKULL HEART LADDER

General Situation: It's no good struggling and trying to do everything on your own. Get your family and friends organized – they'll be only too pleased to lend a hand.

Finance/Business: An outstanding insurance claim or legal wrangle will soon be settled. Invest any money you gain with care.

Love/Affection: You and your partner will find yourselves faced with a decision to make which could either prove to be the best move you've ever made or an absolute disaster.

232 – SKULL HEART LIGHTNING

General Situation: A sudden burst of energy will see you rushing about trying to change everything around you. Make sure that it's only your own life you try to organize. If you meddle with other people's plans you could have problems.

Finance/Business: If faced with something new, consult an expert for advice. Maybe one of your friends is qualified in that particular field – ask. Don't attempt to do anything until you have been properly briefed.

Love/Affection: If you tend to have a roving eye – beware! It could spark off trouble.

231 – SKULL HEART SNAIL

General Situation: Allow yourself more time to relax and keep yourself in good shape. Why not take up some new hobby or interest?

Finance/Business: Avoid making financial decisions at the present time, especially if they are in any way involved with family or friends. Very soon you might need every penny you have and it could be embarrassing if you have to call in loans.

Love/Affection: This should be a quiet and peaceful time for you and your partner. You can both afford to take things easy and relax. Avoid making any decisions, whether major or minor ones. Let them wait until you feel refreshed and ready to deal with them.

226 – SKULL STORK FRUIT-TREE

General Situation: Prepare for some major changes in your life over the next few months. These will be beneficial. They will force you out of your rut and make you start to think for yourself again.

Finance/Business: As far as your career is concerned, the field will be clear for you to surge ahead and promote your own ideas. It could result from the resignation of your greatest rival. Make this opportunity work for you.

Love/Affection: A sudden surge of creative energy will come as quite a surprise to your partner. Instead of wondering when you are going to get around to all the jobs that need doing, they'll be telling you to take it easy and take a break instead.

225 – SKULL STORK GOBLET

General Situation: A good time to tidy up all those odd jobs which you never get around to. Once they're all out of the way you'll be able to devote your time to more relaxing pursuits.

Finance/Business: An error made by a colleague will be to your advantage but resist the temptation to crow over it. Use your own ingenuity and know-how to put matters right.

Love/Affection: Make yourself clearly understood if you are planning something special with your partner. Decide who is to do what if you want your plans to go without a hitch.

224 – SKULL STORK KEY

General Situation: You might be forced to do some rethinking about the course your life is taking. Opportunities are there for you, provided you have sufficient drive and ambition to cope with them.

Finance/Business: Chances for investment might soon arise but beware of schemes with low rates of return. Don't invest more than you can afford to lose.

Love/Affection: There is an offer coming your way which will certainly be worth considering. It could well be the answer to your prayers and it might also solve a lot of problems too.

223 – SKULL STORK LADDER

General Situation: It's time for a good shake-up of anything and everything. Think up a few new ideas or brighten up your old ones. Find something fresh to aim for.

Finance/Business: There could possibly be some confusion over an idea which is primarily yours. Make sure that everyone knows it. Speak up for yourself as there are others only too ready to take the credit.

Love/Affection: You must not allow your partner to manipulate you when faced with a decision you have to make.

222 – SKULL STORK LIGHTNING

General Situation: You will probably have to make a snap decision over something and it could have far-reaching consequences. You may be criticized for your actions but you will be proved right in the long run.

Finance/Business: An unexpected change in your financial affairs will benefit not only you but your immediate family. Take the trouble to explain the situation to them carefully.

Love/Affection: Someone new who will suddenly enter your life could, at first appearances, look to be the one you have been waiting for. Don't do anything hasty – you may have been mistaken.

221 – SKULL STORK SNAIL

General Situation: Try to plan your life so that you have some spare time for relaxation. It's all very well taking on every new opportunity as they arise so long as you are fit enough to cope with it all.

Finance/Business: In order to take on a new financial commitment it will be necessary to take stock of your overall position. See what you really have got, what you could possibly do without and where you can make economies.

Love/Affection: In order to regain your partner's respect and admiration you must try to stand on your own two feet a little more. Try not to be so demanding and become more independent. Not only will it make you more attractive to your partner but it will give you more confidence too.

216 – SKULL SUN FRUIT-TREE

General Situation: If you are feeling happy now, then something new and exciting which could happen soon should leave you feeling positively elated. You will be able to surge ahead and achieve some of the goals you have been aiming for.

Finance/Business: The emphasis for you at the moment is on hard work but not without big rewards at the end of it. Don't allow the odd unexpected surprise or two to take you aback, keep your target in mind and work steadily towards it.

Love/Affection: This is a good time to go into partnership. If you are single then marriage would seem to be indicated – if already married then a joint venture of some kind would be appropriate.

215 – SKULL SUN GOBLET

General Situation: A health problem of long-standing could be much improved by some new form of treatment, bringing with it a new lease of life, more drive and more energy. This is a time when you should enjoy yourself, visit friends or maybe try something different that has not previously been possible.

Finance/Business: Put past mistakes behind you and make the most of what you have. A complete reorganization of your working life is needed. Use your energies to really push for what you want even if it seems that you are reaching too high. You will probably succeed and have cause for celebration. Force the issue by taking the initiative.

Love/Affection: Changes within the family are likely reasons for you to celebrate – maybe a family wedding or christening. If your partner is feeling a little down or undemonstrative, it's up to you to take the lead and cheer him/her up.

214 – SKULL SUN KEY

General Situation: Forget about the past. The future is more important so stop thinking about what might have been. Seize every opportunity that comes your way and work towards something positive and rewarding instead.

Finance/Business: Just because things you have tried to do in the past have failed that's no reason to believe that any new ventures are automatically doomed to failure. Set about solving problems you may have and don't turn down new opportunities on the strength of past misfortunes.

Love/Affection: A few sudden changes will alter the situation between you and your partner and what you make of the situation is entirely up to you. Maybe your children will leave home giving you more time alone together, or a change of residence or occupation could bring about alterations in your lifestyle.

213 – SKULL SUN LADDER

General Situation: If you really want to fulfil a secret ambition then you must take a calm and objective view of everything. Don't allow emotion or a personal bias to cloud the issue as you will only be fooling yourself. An unexpected windfall will also help.

Finance/Business: You could find yourself faced with one or two unforseen expenses which were totally unbudgeted for. Try not to let this dampen your enthusiasm or throw you off course in any way.

Love/Affection: It's about time you two buried the hatched and if you really can't agree about something then find a working compromise instead. Life is too short to be continually arguing so forget your pride and make the first move.

212 – SKULL SUN LIGHTNING

General Situation: Try not to let your mind wander, especially if you are doing something which is potentially dangerous like driving or using an electrically-driven appliance. Accidents happen quickly and most can easily be avoided if a little care is taken.

Finance/Business: Make sure that all your personal possessions or business assets are adequately insured, especially against fire or storm damage. Also make sure that if you have business premises all the safety rules and regulations have been adhered to. A little time spent now could represent money saved later.

Love/Affection: A little unexpected opposition may not be a bad thing as far as your private life is concerned. A good shake-up could be what you need to make you realize just how lucky you are and how much your partner means to you.

211 – SKULL SUN SNAIL

General Situation: An old health problem could flare up again and may well slow you down for a while. Try not to get too despondent if there are things you desperately want to get on with and resist the urge to bore other people with your troubles.

Finance/Business: Not a good time to make any financial moves whether buying or selling. If you do, you could come unstuck as some fairly drastic changes in your economic climate are coming. Far better to watch and wait for the time being.

Love/Affection: If you really want your relationship to survive then you must handle it with great care. Try not to be so dominant and aggressive – show a little more love and consideration and your partner will not fail to respond favourably.

166 – WEB CROSSROADS FRUIT-TREE

General Situation: You may find that new acquaintances you have met are not quite as pleasant as they would have you believe. They may only want to be friendly in order to use you in some way.

Finance/Business: If you have the opportunity to buy something on the cheap, especially a domestic appliance such as a television or washing machine, make sure that everything is above board.

Love/Affection: There's nothing quite like money to spark off rows between husband and wife. If you have spent rather more than you had intended on a hobby or a personal luxury you would be well advised to confess before some interfering neighbour or acquaintance says something precipitous.

165 – WEB CROSSROADS GOBLET

General Situation: At a party or social gathering of some kind you will meet a great many new and intriguing people. However, before you decide to become too involved with any of them, find out just a little bit more about their backgrounds.

Finance/Business: Don't allow the lavish hospitality at a business conference or trade show affect your judgement in any way. These people are only trying to promote themselves and are not really interested in you as a person.

Love/Affection: You could become involved with someone new who you meet at a party or through friends. By all means enjoy their company but be very suspicious if they ask you to do them a big favour almost immediately.

164 – WEB CROSSROADS KEY

General Situation: When opportunity comes knocking at your door make sure you know exactly what risks are involved before you decide to open it. Once you are involved it will be very difficult to back out later.

Finance/Business: If you have any financial difficulties and problems then you must try to solve them by yourself. Once you call in the assistance of other people, especially professionals, you could be letting yourself in for all sorts of unforseen expenses.

Love/Affection: If you and your partner are going through a rough patch at the moment, don't give up. Work together to put matters right. Whatever you do, avoid pouring your heart out to a complete stranger, however sympathetic they may seem, it could make matters worse.

163 – WEB CROSSROADS LADDER

General Situation: If you want to better yourself and really get on, then take the trouble to look at others and find out how they have managed it. Talk to them and learn from their mistakes.

Finance/Business: Try not to get too caught up in other people's enthusiasm. Something which may be very easy and profitable for them may not be half so easy for you and could be a financial disaster too. Watch and admire if you must but don't get involved yourself.

Love/Affection: If you are being deceptive and underhand you can be sure that your partner will find you out – one way or another. There's always someone only too ready to pass on a bit of gossip.

162 – WEB CROSSROADS LIGHTNING

General Situation: Life is full of surprises and a foreigner, who you will shortly meet, could have one or two for you – especially if you ask them into your home and introduce them to your family.

Finance/Business: Don't be in too much of a rush to get involved in a business deal which has overseas connections. Acquaint yourself with all the rules and regulations concerning foreign business.

Love/Affection: Whatever you do, don't allow yourself to become involved in the domestic arguments of a neighbour or friend. Lending a sympathetic ear is one thing, but proffering advice could land you in trouble.

161 – WEB CROSSROADS SNAIL

General Situation: If you have reached the point when you feel you could do with a break and get away from everything for a few days, think carefully before you decide where to go. Don't just turn up unannounced on friends, however well you know them or you could arrive in the middle of a domestic crisis.

Finance/Business: Think very carefully before you decide to lend anyone money. It could well be the last you see of it. Far wiser to say no and risk offence than to say yes and be the loser.

Love/Affection: Should you hear some gossip concerning your partner, don't allow it to colour your feelings for them. Confront them openly with what you have heard and hear their side of the story.

156 – WEB CAT FRUIT-TREE

General Situation: Most families have a black sheep – and should he or she turn up unannounced, make sure that everything is kept on a very friendly footing and that old feuds and grievances, especially about money, are kept well out of the conversation.

Finance/Business: If you are involved with family trust funds or wills, especially if you are named as executor, make sure that everything is properly organized.

Love/Affection: If you and your partner have recently come into some money, make sure that he/she gets their fair share or you could find yourself unjustly accused of trickery. Don't fall out over money.

155 – WEB CAT GOBLET

General Situation: Avoid turning down an invitation to a family gathering because you don't think you'll enjoy it. Go along, enter into the spirit of things and you'll be surprised how much you'll benefit.

Finance/Business: If you are expected to pay a large bill for something like a wedding, try to keep costs down as much as possible. There is a chance you could waste a great deal.

Love/Affection: If you and your family do not always see eye to eye about your choice of partner, don't allow them to involve you in a public argument over the subject. This applies especially if you will shortly be attending a social function at which other members of your family will be present.

154 – WEB CAT KEY

General Situation: If you can see that a member of your family is about to get involved in something rather risky then give them the benefit of your experience and point out the pitfalls to them. They may choose to totally ignore your wisdom but, at least, you will know that you did try to warn them.

Finance/Business: If you have any financial worries that you find difficult to cope with, it might be a good idea to talk things over with your family to see what they can come up with. You might be able to unravel the problem between you.

Love/Affection: If you are looking for a way to wriggle out of an entanglement which is becoming more and more involved, seek advice from a relative who has been in a similar situation and may be able to help. Once you have decided how to handle matters, wait for the right moment to act.

153 – WEB CAT LADDER

General Situation: Try not to let your family interfere in your personal ambitions however well-meaning they may be. Listen to the advice they offer, it could well be good, but in the long run you must decide what's going to be done and how you want to do it.

Finance/Business: You must think very carefully about all the disadvantages before you decide to run a business from home. You may save the time usually spent travelling and economize on outgoings but what about the distractions? – children, pets, callers, household chores. It could be disastrous for your concentration.

Love/Affection: Don't let family squabbles and petty jealousies come between you and your partner. And don't let your family encroach on your spare time!

152 – WEB CAT LIGHTNING

General Situation: If you are involved in something which your family are unaware of and which they would strongly disapprove of, you had better tie up any loose ends without delay if you wish to avoid detection. Or better still – confess the whole affair and clear your conscience.

Finance/Business: Hang on to your money and avoid buying frivolous items.

Love/Affection: Sharing your life with someone is not quite so easy as it seems and if you want it to succeed you will have to give as well as take. So don't be surprised, if you do something inconsiderate once too often, that you find yourself at the centre of a row.

151 – WEB CAT SNAIL

General Situation: Beware of hidden problems. You can only overcome them by approaching all matters with caution at the moment.

Finance/Business: Be careful if you are tempted to invest in an 'antique'. It's very easy to make mistakes.

Love/Affection: Don't allow your partner to draw you into an argument concerning either your family or his/hers. Proceed with care – don't take sides, and change the subject if at all possible.

146 – WEB KNIFE FRUIT-TREE

General Situation: Not a good time for you at the moment. Everything you have worked for seems to be vulnerable and at risk. But try not to get too depressed and don't make any hasty, snap decisions. Don't let your own carelessness involve you in an accident.

Finance/Business: The night of the long knives! Workplace politics, crafty dealings and confusion are rife. Even your job or financial position could be in jeopardy. Avoid any decisions until you know who you can trust, and don't underwrite anyone else's schemes as this could bring problems.

Love/Affection: Possibly someone close to you is up to something a little underhand and, although you can sense something wrong, it will be very hard to identify the problem. All you can do is keep your ears and eyes open and try not to say things you might later regret if drawn into an argument. It is especially important that you do not quarrel over money.

145 – WEB KNIFE GOBLET

General Situation: Definitely not a good time to go filling your diary with social engagements of any kind at all. There may be safety in numbers but right now the greater the number the greater the risk of deception, guile, insincerity and duplicity. Stay at home with a good book.

Finance/Business: There's something slightly underhand going on around you so keep your ears open and see what information you can pick up that might be to your advantage. Don't act on it too quickly.

Love/Affection: Your partner probably has a lot to put up with having you as his/her other half. Relax more and stop seeing problems where none exist.

144 – WEB KNIFE KEY

General Situation: Don't allow plotting and scheming by others around you to spoil your chances. Keep your sights set firmly on your own objectives and do the best you can.

Finance/Business: Industrial disputes could cause you heavy financial losses either directly or indirectly. You must try to find a way to reopen communications between management and unions.

Love/Affection: If your private affairs seem to be in a state of turmoil and you don't really know what to do for the best, then do nothing. Let matters ride for a while longer even if you are really discontented – time has its own way of solving problems if you are only prepared to wait long enough.

143 – WEB KNIFE LADDER

General Situation: Try to maintain a calm exterior even if you are feeling liable to explode at any moment. Losing your temper will only make you appear foolish. Get a firm grip on yourself and deal with your problems one by one.

Finance/Business: Try not to be so easily discouraged and defeatist. Don't be manipulated and downtrodden – you will need all your courage and determination to succeed.

Love/Affection: The presence of a new colleague of the opposite sex will prove to be a great distraction and also something of a temptation. It really depends upon how good a relationship you have with your partner at present as to how you act.

142 – WEB KNIFE LIGHTNING

General Situation: If you are prepared to act quickly then you will soon be able to solve a major problem in your life. Don't expect that this will be an easy course to take because it will not. You'll have to work hard and put all your skills to the test. Are you up to the challenge, and can you put other temptations aside?

Finance/Business: Try to be as independent as you possibly can and don't rely so much on other people to get you out of difficulties. If you consider matters carefully and do not do anything rash you should be able to avoid most financial pitfalls. Be more confident.

Love/Affection: Even though someone you are very fond of seems to be making rather a mess of their lives you must not get involved in their problems if you value that friendship. Any offer of help or advice from you could be totally misunderstood. Be prepared to pick up the pieces if necessary, but don't interfere.

141 – WEB KNIFE SNAIL

General Situation: Do not allow the friction and feuding of those around you to undermine your own health. Their arguments are no concern of yours. Lend a sympathetic ear if you think it might help but don't get trapped into taking sides. You must remain neutral.

Finance/Business: Financially you are best advised to make no moves at all until new guidelines have been established.

Love/Affection: Resist the temptation to involve yourself in matchmaking – however well-suited you may think the two people are. It's a bad idea to manipulate people, however good your intentions may be.

136 – WEB HEART FRUIT-TREE

General Situation: Make sure that, when you are out and about with friends, you're not always the one who has to foot the bill. You work hard for the money you earn so be on the lookout for others only too ready to spend it for you.

Finance/Business: One of your so-called 'friends' at work, who you thought you could trust, is about to show him/herself in their true colours. Their activities will soon be discovered. Don't let yourself be labelled guilty by association.

Love/Affection: Don't try to impress someone special in your life by putting on an act and trying to be something you're not. Far better to be yourself than risk being exposed as a fraud at a later date.

135 – WEB HEART GOBLET

General Situation: Get out of the rat race for a while and try to spend more time with your family and friends. You'll be able to relax in the company of people you trust instead of having to keep on your toes in case someone is after your job or checking up on you to make sure that you are doing it properly.

Finance/Business: If some pet project of yours at work (or a hobby) which has cost you considerable sums of money doesn't seem to be succeeding or as fulfilling as you had hoped – then write it off. Any more you spend on it will be wasted.

Love/Affection: If your emotional encounters have been disappointing recently and you are feeling a bit down and unloved, then why not look up some old friends and find out what they have been up to lately.

134 – WEB HEART KEY

General Situation: If you feel that life is somehow passing you by and that you would like to live a little more, get out and about. The chances are that new interests will bring you the opportunities you are looking for.

Finance/Business: You should try to show a little more care when handling your own affairs. Make sure that you don't get short-changed when out shopping and lending money, to even your closest friend, is inadvisable and could cause problems.

Love/Affection: Honesty is the best policy, whether married or single, if you want to get the best out of a relationship. Avoid being underhand in any way.

133 – WEB HEART LADDER

General Situation: New opportunities are coming your way which could bring great successes. However, try to reach your goal by honest methods or you could lose a few friends on the way.

Finance/Business: If you are thinking of applying for a new job, particularly one where a friend could put in a good word for you, make sure that you have the necessary qualifications. You'll be wasting everyone's time if the position is beyond your capabilities and your friend will be made to look foolish too.

Love/Affection: Put your own hobbies and interests to one side and spend more of your leisure time with your partner. It will improve your relationship and you can always go back to them at a later date.

132 – WEB HEART LIGHTNING

General Situation: Try to avoid doing anything rash at the moment. Your family and friends are sure to misunderstand your motives.

Finance/Business: Should a really good opportunity arise to make some money quickly, don't waste time seeking advice but act fast and let your own feelings be your guide on this occasion.

Love/Affection: If you want to keep your partner's love and trust, then don't go discussing your private affairs with other people. Not everyone can keep confidences to themselves and the last thing you both want are others gossiping about you behind your backs. You should sort out your own problems between you.

131 – WEB HEART SNAIL

General Situation: Someone who you are very fond of is overdoing it and you know it. Try to make them take things easier and help them whenever you can as they seem to have a lot on their plate at present.

Finance/Business: Try to avoid making decisions concerning money if at all possible. Play for time while you check the situation. By using delaying tactics you could spot something going on which you might otherwise not have noticed.

Love/Affection: Show a little more compassion for your partner – he/she may not really be feeling well but is doing his/her best to hide it from you. Go out of your way to lend a hand and make sure that they take it easy until they are fully recovered.

126 – WEB STORK FRUIT-TREE

General Situation: Now is the time to plan improvements for both home and work. Be more creative and imaginative, but resist the temptation to wander off into the realms of fantasy – your schemes must be feasible.

Finance/Business: If your talents and creative abilities are not fully appreciated where you work at present, consider applying for another job or even becoming self-employed. There are some drawbacks to this but if you have half the ability and resourcefulness you think you have, then you'll survive.

Love/Affection: Where your private life is concerned, try to forget about past involvements as they are over and done with – brooding won't help. Instead, try to concentrate on your future and work hard at it. Above all, don't go making the same mistakes all over again, you should have learned your lesson by now.

125 – WEB STORK GOBLET

General Situation: Life for you will soon improve dramatically and you will be involved in the organization of an important project. This could be the chance you have been waiting for to try out new ideas and concepts. Be creative and don't be afraid to experiment.

Finance/Business: Don't be in too much of a hurry to spend all your spare money on a hobby or entertainment but keep a little back for a rainy day. You'll be glad that you did as the opportunity to tackle something new could soon present itself and you will certainly need the money then.

Love/Affection: As far as personal affairs are concerned, this could be a very unsettled and confusing time for you. This period will soon pass.

124 – WEB STORK KEY

General Situation: Your chance to use your imagination and flair for organization is coming and it will certainly get you out of the rut you are in. Important and influential people will become involved in your life and will be of great assistance to you, both now and in the future.

Finance/Business: It is likely that you will be invited to join some form of professional or business partnership very soon. Treat this offer with some caution, especially if you are required to invest your own money in the venture.

Love/Affection: Try not to spend so much of your time worrying about the stability of your relationship with your partner. There is really no need.

123 – WEB STORK LADDER

General Situation: If you dream of advancement, go ahead and try – you are quite capable of achieving success. Handle people with care and consideration – you may need their help one day.

Finance/Business: Before embarking on any new schemes, make sure that they really are viable propositions.

Love/Affection: Find the time to talk to your partner in private and make sure that his/her dreams and aspirations really are the same as yours before getting involved in long-term schemes. You could be surprised at the answers you get.

122 – WEB STORK LIGHTNING

General Situation: Avoid putting too many irons in the fire at once and resist the temptation to take on more than you can comfortably handle. This will only cause confusion and carelessness.

Finance/Business: Don't allow other people to take advantage of your good nature. You will be the one who takes the blame if things go wrong and besides, you really haven't the time to spare. You should have enough work of your own to fully occupy your time.

Love/Affection: If your partner is putting some kind of pressure on you to reach a quick decision over a personal matter, try to delay for as long as possible. This will give you time to think things over.

121 – WEB STORK SNAIL

General Situation: Although you may be feeling at the peak of physical condition you should take care of your health. Any strenuous activities, especially a new sport, should be approached carefully.

Finance/Business: Financially this is a time for taking stock of your resources, thinking and planning but not doing. If you go over your plans for the future carefully and meticulously you should be able to spot potential trouble spots.

Love/Affection: If the stresses and strains of everyday life have been getting you down lately and your plans and ideas have been beset with problems and complications, then talk things over with your partner. The love and concern they show for you will have a stabilizing effect on you.

116 – WEB SUN FRUIT-TREE

General Situation: Try not to get sidetracked if you want to make headway and achieve a personal ambition. There will be plenty of time later to do other things, but right now you must drive yourself on and reach your goal.

Finance/Business: If you want to avoid financial disaster you must learn to live within your means and stop pretending that you are better off than you really are. Take stock of your situation and see where economies can be made.

Love/Affection: Money, success and the power that goes with it can attract the wrong sort of people. Try to play down your achievements and don't make such a show of your possessions.

115 – WEB SUN GOBLET

General Situation: Don't fall into the old trap of saying more than you mean when relaxed and off your guard. Alcohol not only loosens your tongue but it also impairs your judgement – avoid discussing your private affairs over a round of drinks.

Finance/Business: Your drive and ambitious nature could be responsible for your promotion at work. However, try not to count your chickens too soon.

Love/Affection: If you are not careful you could find yourself, through no fault of your own, in a very complicated situation involving a divorcee you will meet at a party or social gathering. Handle this delicate problem with kid gloves or you could stir up all sorts of trouble for both yourself and your family.

114 – WEB SUN KEY

General Situation: You seem to have a natural talent for helping others to overcome their problems and difficulties. However, you must remember that when you become involved in other people's affairs you may sometimes become privvy to confidential information. Don't repeat what you hear.

Finance/Business: You already have the key to your financial success although you may not have known how to use it before. You can listen and you can speak and that's just what you must do. Listen to other people who have done well for themselves and hear how they did it.

Love/Affection: You can't go on playing the field for ever and although you may have narrowed it down to two runners, you still have to make a choice soon or you could end up with no-one. Choose the one who makes you happy.

113 – WEB SUN LADDER

General Situation: Honesty is always the best policy so don't be tempted to say you can do something when you know in your heart that it's beyond you. You are sure to get caught out at some point and could ruin your chances for the future.

Finance/Business: Now is the time to 'pull your socks up' before it's too late and double your efforts. The choice is yours.

Love/Affection: You and your partner will soon find yourselves working together very hard on something which you both share a passion for – this could well be renovating an old house. You are both extremely determined people when you set your minds on something and are sure to succeed. Watch out, however, for minor snags and pitfalls which could slow your progress.

112 – WEB SUN LIGHTNING

General Situation: You will have to act quickly if you want to make the most of an opportunity you will soon be offered. Rapid and accurate calculations will also be called for as you won't have time to recheck anything later on.

Finance/Business: Don't sign or commit yourself to anything unless you are properly in the picture and have had everything explained to you.

Love/Affection: Try not to be quite so self-centred for a change, your career won't fall into ruins if you take a night off and relax with your partner. Don't be quite so serious all the time.

111 – WEB SUN SNAIL

General Situation: Plan to spend an entire day doing nothing except enjoying yourself or have a lazy time with friends. All those important, complicated tasks which you ought to be getting on with will still be there but today you should unwind and take it easy.

Finance/Business: Try to keep your financial dealings as simple and as uncomplicated as possible if you want to avoid unnecessary worry and stress. The more complex you allow your dealings to become the more you increase the risk of confusion and trouble. Practise simplicity for peace of mind.

Love/Affection: If there are subjects not for discussion in your relationship, which you know are potential trouble spots, such as money, religion, relatives and so on, then steer clear of them if you want to avoid complications. Collect your thoughts before you speak and that way your relationship should stay happy and successful.

Of further interest

The Prediction Tarot Pack
SASHA FENTON

The ideal pack for Tarot enthusiasts and beginners alike contains:

The Prediction Tarot Deck, a hauntingly beautiful set of 78 full-colour Tarot cards conceived by Bernard Stringer and painted by Peter Richardson. The simplicity of their design makes it an ideal deck to use for fortune-telling.

Fortune-Telling by Tarot Cards, a special edition of the best-selling primer by professional Tarot reader and author Sasha Fenton. The book provides a straightforward yet comprehensive guide to the art of reading and interpreting Tarot cards.

As individual items, each has sold over 100,000 copies. Together they make a unique package which will enable anyone to embark upon a voyage of discovery into the world of Tarot.

Available from HarperCollins Distribution Services,
P.O. Box Glasgow G4 0NB
Telephone: 0141 772 3200   Fax: 0141 762 0584
Price: £20.00   ISBN: 0 850 30476 8